Praise for Ben a

"Ben Loeb, while paying attention to what science-minded sport psychology professionals have to say, pulls from years of practical experience as a coach and as a parent. His text illuminates practical strategies to bridge theory and practice, providing athletes, coaches, and others with approaches that should feel tangible to everyone."

Tim Herzog, EdD, CMPC

Reaching Ahead Counseling and Mental Performance

"Ben Loeb has packed a lifetime of experience into an easy-to-follow game plan that will help any athlete or team maximize their potential. Each chapter contains clear, concise content as well as assets to stimulate thinking, activities for application, and exploratory exercises to take away and put into practice. This is a great tool for coaches at every level!"

Sherri Coale

Author, Speaker, Hall of Fame Coach (University of Oklahoma 1996-2021)

"Ben Loeb's book *Grow Your Game* provides insightful guidance on mental performance and team development. With a wealth of experience and a commitment to continuous learning, Coach Loeb offers valuable advice on fostering lasting team cultures through shared values and a 'we' language approach. A necessary read for anyone looking to enhance their performance on and off the court."

Emma Doyle

Performance Coach and Author of What Makes a Great Coach?

"I had the privilege of working with Coach Loeb and his tennis team in the fall 2023 season. Coach Loeb is the ultimate positive coach who leads with a growth mindset and is invested in the holistic development of each one of his athletes. This book reflects his admirable character and love of the process for achieving personal and team excellence. I recommend to all who are committed to growing their game!"

Dr. Scotta Morton

Go For It Coaching, LLC, Mental Performance Coach

"Ben's *Grow Your Game* is a great example of blending the art of coaching with the science of sport psychology. His direct, practical advice, drawn from extensive experience, offers clear pathways for athletes and coaches alike to elevate their performance. This book goes beyond theoretical knowledge, providing tangible strategies and exercises that can be applied immediately."

Duncan Simpson, PhD, CMPC,

Director, Personal Development - IMG Academy

"*Grow Your Game* is a wonderful resource for athletes and coaches that want to get to the next level with their sport or performance area. Coach Loeb has put together a comprehensive, A-Z blueprint to develop the mental skills and toughness to perform at peak potential. I highly recommend *Grow Your Game* to any high achiever committed to be at their best. It will help you transform on and off the court and in other aspects of your life."

Jeff Salzenstein

Success Coach, Speaker, and Former Top 100 World Ranked Tennis Player

"As a longtime colleague of Ben's, I have witnessed his passion firsthand as it pertains to the mental skill development for athletes in any performance endeavor. This book houses many applicable principles and serves as a valuable resource for athletes and coaches alike."

Neal Blackburn

Rock Bridge High School Track & Cross Country Head Coach
Missouri Track & Cross Country Coaches' Association Hall of Fame

GROW YOUR GAME

GROW YOUR GAME

100 Mental Performance Exercises and Reflections to Be a Better Player and Teammate

BEN LOEB, Ed. S

Printed in the United States of America.
First edition 2024.

Cover and layout design by G Sharp Design, LLC.
www.gsharpmajor.com

ISBN 979-8-9906290-0-4 (paperback)
ISBN 979-8-9906290-1-1 (ebook)

A Note About the Cover Designs
The three primary schools where I have coached tennis teams are acknowledged with their school colors shown on the front and/or back cover of the book.

- Rock Bridge High School, the most impactful of my coaching career, with the green and gold (1994-2024+).

- Hickman High School, critical formative years to start my high school coaching career, with the purple and gold (1989-1994).

- The University of Missouri-Columbia, the foundational start of my coaching career, with the black and gold (1986-1988).

This acknowledgment represents a thank you to the student-athletes that have enriched my life, as I hope I have enriched theirs.

This book is dedicated to my son, Ben Loeb. Ben played on the Rock Bridge High School Tennis Team in Columbia, MO in 2021 and 2022. When Ben first started practicing before the 2021 season, I thought he would be at the low end of the junior varsity. Ben showed great perseverance, commitment, and a mentally strong competitive spirit, to earn a starting varsity position on the team. He then moved up the rank order during the season. The team finished fourth in the large school class in Missouri State Tennis. What I value the most is that I got the opportunity to coach my son in high school athletics. I'm so thankful for that time in my life.

CONTENTS

PREFACE

People learn by doing, not just by listening to a coach give their philosophy or by solely reading something. This mental performance coaching manual is designed for the athlete (and coach, if applicable) to self-reflect on each exercise or statement. Then, to respond to the question(s) with the intent of discovering how the answers impact the athlete's life on or off the athletic court or field.

Each chapter has a minimum of eight exercises and/or reflections as they relate to the topic. The intent is for an athlete to do some of the exercises in each chapter but not all of them during a given season. The athlete or coach can track which ones they have done and then next season either repeat some of them and/or do new exercises. Another approach is to focus on a particular topic or two and do more exercises from those chapters.

The key is for the athlete to participate in their personal journey for self-discovery by doing the exercises. It is one thing to read something. It takes it to another level to read, reflect, and then implement. The action step of implementation is essential for personal growth. That's how you grow your game.

It is best for the athletes to share with each other in a team setting. There may be times a coach can guide team members through exercises and say very little. The athlete doing and then sharing will teach them plenty. There are other times a coach may do more sharing of their philosophical beliefs on the topic exercise.

In most cases there is no need for everyone to share with the whole group (i.e., team), unless you have a small group, because it might take too long. Have them share in groups of two or three people. Then the coach might call on a few team members to share with the whole group. If you are working on this as an individual, share with a parent, with your individual coach, or with a close friend.

I have researched, studied, and most notably applied mental performance improvement strategies with the tennis teams I have coached for nearly 40 years. I also developed and taught a sport psychology course at the high school level for nine years (2011 through 2019). I have incorporated mental performance exercises and reflective thoughts into my coaching throughout my career.

This manual is a way to share some of these exercises with people in a competitive sports arena. Choose which exercise titles sound appealing to you. I think you will find them quite useful.

Check out my website: **https://benloebcoaching.com** for books, blog posts, and reflections, plus tennis instructional videos that I have done.

Congratulations on investing in yourself. It's a worthy venture.

CHAPTER 1

TEAM BUILDING

Introduction to Team Building

The "*What*":

Team Building is the development and sharing of team expectations and core values that will help guide team members toward a shared vision. It is important to have a coach and/or team leaders that will help direct team members to buy into the team expectations and core values.

The "*Why*":

Both leadership and player buy-in help create a positive team culture that creates a moral compass for the team to follow. Team cohesion, accountability, and integrity create a team environment that is favorable for maximizing team success and enjoyment of the team bonding experience.

The "*How*":

Team members need to be educated on what team dynamics look like. Educate team members on the "We" vs "Me" mentality. Use reminders during the season with the whole team and with individuals that need some one-on-one consultation. The goal is that education and reminders will lead to desired team interaction and team commitment.

The following exercises will give you specific opportunities to improve team building.

CARE Team Expectations - Are You Willing to CARE Along the Journey?

C - Committed
A - Accountable
R - Respectful
E - Enthusiastic

C - are you committed to the group by making practice time a priority (i.e., preparation, timeliness to practice/ duration, effort)?

A - are you accountable for your level of performance and your results?

R - are you respectful of your teammates and coaches (i.e., communication, coachability)?

E - are you enthusiastic about your involvement with the team and do you show a positive attitude?

Team Journey Statement—You may not know where the journey will take you, but you do have control over how much you CARE.

How will you show you "CARE" about the team journey for the coming season? You may refer to aspects of the acronym or address the question by how you will be team-oriented in other ways...

Core Values: The Foundation of a Team Culture

1. **Establish** 4 foundational core values that exemplify the shared vision of your team.
2. **Define** the core values and then review them periodically (discuss their meaning).
3. **Live** the established core values together to create a more enriching team experience.

Listed below are the team core values we have used for the high school tennis teams I have coached over the past several years. You can change some of them from year to year or keep them the same.

Our core values are: (1) Respect; (2) Teamwork; (3) Commitment; (4) Fighting Spirit

Core Value #1: _______________________________________

Defined:

Core Value #2: _______________________________________

Defined:

Core Value #3: _______________________________________

Defined:

Core Value #4: _______________________________________

Defined:

How often will your team review your core values?

____weekly ____ bi-weekly (two weeks) ____monthly

Cultivating a Team Environment That Maximizes Performance

There are three types of team environments that a team member prefers, according to Jeff Moore, a leadership consultant who has studied personal attributes as they relate to the work or team environment. The three types of environments are:

1) Cooperative; 2) Collaborative; and 3) Competitive.[1]

Cooperative Environment - The player wants autonomy and certainty in the environment (i.e., playing time, with whom they practice etc.). They accept direction and then they want autonomy in how to do it. They want to "co-operate," meaning operate as an individual within the context of the group. They prefer a stable environment with independence and a low risk of change. In this environment the level of competitive interaction is basically none.

Collaborative Environment - The player is comfortable dealing with some uncertainty in the environment and they value working together with teammates. Team harmony, where everyone gets along, is important to this type of player. They are comfortable with a moderate level of risk regarding changes in their environment. The level of competitive interaction is relatively low.

1 Jeff Moore. Texas Tennis Coaches Association Convention. "Building a Championship Team versus a Winning Team." Follow-up at **www.mooreleadership.com**

Competitive Environment - The player thrives in ambiguity and is not worried about uncertainty in the environment. In this environment, the word "compete" means to strive together. The player realizes you need to compete against each other and with each other (i.e., teammates in a scrimmage), yet still support each other outside of the competitive process. This player is willing to accept a higher level of risk of change in the environment. The player likes to work with others, but they feel a need for a moderate or higher level of competitive interaction in the environment.

Which environment do you prefer? Why?

Which environment is best to maximize your team's potential? Why?

Discuss your responses with a teammate, your coach, and/or your team.

"We Will" Statements for Team Goal Setting

Team Goals

These are shared goals that team members will strive together in how they approach goal attainment. These shared goals lead us to what we want to accomplish. These "We Will" statements are the intentions we buy into that will improve the chances of us reaching our team goals.

First, set a team goal (performance goal or outcome goal). Then write the **"We Will" Statement(s)** for reaching that team goal. These are the action statements or process goals to reach the team goal.

Team Goal:

____

____

Review these action statements weekly to guide you to accomplish your team goal.

We will:

We will:

We will:

Review these statements weekly to guide you to accomplish your team goal.

Dates reviewed:

________ ________ ________ ________

Hero-Hardship-Highlight[2]

Identify an example of each of the following in your life. Then share it with a team member and/ or with the team.

Hero - Who is a hero of yours and why?

Hardship - Identify a hardship you have been through and how it has impacted your life.

Highlight - What is a highlight for you in your life? What is an accomplishment that you will always remember?

2 Larissa Anderson, University of Missouri Softball Coach.

Team Culture: Why Is It So Important?

A team's culture is made up of the values, beliefs, attitudes, and behaviors shared by a team. It's how people work together towards a common goal and how they treat each other. These attributes could be positive or negative.

A good culture is one in which team members collaborate and support one another. Teams that do not have a good team culture need an abundance of precise rules and regulations. Where a culture is strong, trust exists, and people will choose to do the right thing.

How do you build a strong team culture?

Everyone must take ownership and act as a united team. This is a lot easier if you have good leadership on the team.

List some attributes that will make for a strong team culture on your team:

Team Cohesion: How Can You Promote It?

There is more to team dynamics than how much the individual members like each other. It is possible for teammates to not have a close connection with each other and still win. Most coaches and athletes prefer teammates to like each other, but it is not imperative as long as they remain focused on their common task and share the same goals and beliefs.

Coaches and players could work on developing good team communication and shared responsibility—developing the 'we' mentality. The 'we' mentality can raise the performance of all the players in a team and help reduce the pressure associated with big games. Listed below are some of the key attributes of an effective team. Notice they are task-oriented and have nothing to do with social relationships.

- A common vision
- Clear and definite goals that support the vision.
- Players who put the common good before their own interests
- Players who take responsibility and who are accountable for their performance.
- Players that realize that mistakes are part of the game.

Question:

Name at least one factor from the list above that is important for team cohesion on your team and explain why.

Team Building: Reflections

Great Teams Are Made Of...

"Great teams are made of individual athletes who have given up their quest for personal glory, who have willingly and wholeheartedly embraced the character traits of a team player and who have fully committed themselves to the group effort. These players will come to understand one of life's great lessons; they will be a stronger individual if they have experienced being part of a great team."

Bruce Brown, author, *Great Teams: The Seven Essentials*

Team Dynamics

"You have to handle things. You don't hold grudges against people. You just work through it. Because, if you don't... then you just have two sides going against each other. And that's not what you want. You preach being a team. Those are the things you want to continue to hold on to. Things happen. You just work through it and work on to the next thing. Move forward."

Jack Flaherty, pitcher, St. Louis Cardinals

What Lessons Have Your Players Learned?

"Accountability—being accountable for whatever you do and to the people around you."

(Note: Accountability defined as the acceptance of responsibility for one's own actions)

"Integrity—doing what you're supposed to do when no one else is watching."

Bev Buckley, Rollins College Women's Tennis Coach

Self vs Team

"No prize won for self can compare to the great feeling of accomplishment and pride that's shared in victory among those who've suffered side by side for a common cause."

Anonymous

What is it about team competition that is so inspiring for you?

Team Chemistry is Built By

"Team chemistry is built by being part of something bigger than yourself. You cultivate team chemistry by being open and getting the group to be aligned. It takes player ownership, accountability, and leadership. The group is open and receptive to brutally honest, hard messages. I'm very direct but by no means disrespectful or hurtful. I think that is what the players like whether it be good or bad messages."

Bradley Carnell, head coach, St. Louis City SC (MLS)

CHAPTER 2
CONFIDENCE

Introduction to Confidence

The "*What*":

Confidence is a firm belief in oneself.

The "*Why*":

Confidence is important because you must have it, particularly in crunch time, to bring out the best in yourself. With confidence you can trust yourself to perform. Without it, you can get in your own way with doubt and overthinking.

The "How":

Improved confidence will come from monitoring your thoughts and feelings about yourself. You can redirect your thoughts with your self-talk. You can modify your feelings with how you see yourself (self-image). When you look in the mirror, see the person you either respect and admire or the person you aspire to be. See setbacks as temporary, rather than as a permanent, negative label that defines you.

The following exercises will give you specific opportunities to improve your confidence.

What Is the Best Way to Build Confidence? Take a CAP Approach

1. **Competitive Traits**: Know the competitive traits you admire in others and you instill in yourself. Examples of competitive traits that can create a better sense of confidence include sustained effort, positive attitude, resilience, fighting spirit, mental toughness, and emotional strength. Be determined to live up to the competitive traits that inspire you and guide you.

   List two competitive traits that you want to define you:

2. **Acknowledgement:** Acknowledge your fears or insecurities. Seek to understand the origin of them. Then re-program your thinking with conviction to be more supportive of yourself (i.e., self-talk).

   List a fear or insecurity that you have:

3. **Personal Growth:** Accept your emotions. When you're learning how to be more confident, it's tempting to focus on your "ideal self"—the person you wish you were. Instead, focus on who you are, value your own self-worth, and see your ability for personal growth and achievement.

   What is one way you can grow into being more confident or to maintain a high level of confidence?

Confidence vs Anxiety

Confidence comes from **the belief** that your **resources** are **greater** than the **demands**.

Anxiety comes from **the belief** that the **demands** are **greater** than your **resources**.

List a couple resources (i.e., strengths) you have to perform in the upper range of your capabilities:

List a couple demands (i.e., psychological blocks or opponent concerns) you perceive that will test your resources:

What beliefs do you need to perceive your resources can overcome the demands?

Confidence Is a Choice

Repeating an affirmation to yourself will not in itself change your mental state.

What 's going to change your mental state of being from self-doubt or nervousness to being relaxed and confident is you making the choice to be that way. It takes more than good physical practice habits to attain true confidence. Your mental/emotional state of being, affected by thoughts and feelings, goes a long way toward being able to truly choose confidence.

Create the state of being you want, and from that place, your actions should be in alignment with being confident.

What tips should you give yourself to develop a confident mindset?

Confidence and Trust in Competition: "The Freeze Factor"

To what degree do you freeze up in real game competition against an opponent as compared to competition during practice? Some players freeze up mentally (lack confidence) or they freeze up physically (lack trust).

The difference between confidence and trust is confidence stems from how strongly you believe you can perform well. Trust is the ability to be on "autopilot," whereby you rely on physical movement memory to execute a motor skill.

Circle the number below that indicates your self-evaluation in both practice scrimmaging and in competition. The continuum goes from very low freeze up (maintain confidence and trust) to very high freeze up (lack confidence and trust). The players that have more confidence, and the ability to trust themselves when needed most, self-score at the lower end of the scale.

The "Freeze Factor'

	Very Low				Very High
Practice:	1	2	3	4	5
Real Game:	1	2	3	4	5

It's important to trust your physical skills and abilities. The trust comes from having confidence in your ability to meet the demands before you. It's essential that you are not only able, but also willing, to perform spontaneously (physically) and intuitively (mentally) when you are in challenging situations. Do the following to help you get into a mental state to perform in the upper range of your capabilities.

1. **Identify** your fears and then determine how you will manage them.
2. **Visualize** how you will deal with challenging situations in competition by using your new found perspective in managing fear.
3. **Show** self-acceptance, accountability, and resilience when things don't go your way.

Here are some final thoughts on how you can perform better with confidence and trust:

- Trust your technique while in the process of doing (see-react-play)
- Play in the present moment (perform in the now, unconcerned about "what ifs")
- Realize mistakes are part of the game. Perfectionism is a losing game.
- How you see yourself is more important than concerns about how others perceive you if you don't succeed.

Life in the "freezer" is uncomfortable. Create your own sunshine and warmth by believing in yourself. Show confidence and trust in your own abilities.

The Confidence Challenge[3]

It's easy to stay confident when you're performing well, when the conditions are ideal, and when you're competing against someone you're better than.

The real test of confidence, however, is how you respond when things aren't going your way. Dr. Jim Taylor, an authority on the psychology of performance in business, sport, and parenting, calls this "the Confidence Challenge."[4] He explains that what separates the best athletes from the rest is that the best are able to maintain their confidence when they're not at the top of their game. By staying confident, they continue to work hard instead of giving up, because they know that their performance will come around in time.

Most athletes who perform poorly get caught in the vicious cycle of low confidence and low performance. Low performance leads to low confidence, which leads to a continuation of low performance and low confidence. Once you slip into that downward spiral, you rarely can get out of it in the short term. It's tough to get off that no fun merry-go-round.

In contrast, athletes with prime confidence can ride out the downward flows of the game and seek out ways to return to their previous level. Prime confidence is a deep, lasting, and resilient belief in one's ability. All athletes will go through periods when they don't perform well. The skill is not getting caught in the vicious cycle and being able to get out of the down periods quickly.

3 Ben Loeb, *Next Level Coaching*

4 Dr. Jim Taylor, **https://www.drjimtaylor.com/4.0/sports-introduction-to-confidence/**

There are several keys to mastering the Confidence Challenge. **Circle the number for which statements you find challenging:**

1. Develop the attitude that demanding situations are challenges that should be sought out.
2. Be well prepared to meet challenges (adequate practice preparation).
3. Stay positive and motivated in the face of difficulties.
4. Focus on what you need to do to overcome challenges (problem-centric vs solution-centric).
5. Accept that you may experience failure when faced with new challenges.
6. Never give up! And don't withdraw effort (i.e., "tank") when the going gets tough.

Confidence Challenge Goal Statement

Select one of the numbers above that you want to improve on as a confidence challenge. Then write a CC Goal Statement. You may add an action step if applicable. For instance, "I will stay positive and motivated in the face of difficulties by utilizing positve self-talk." Review your CC Goal Statement periodically or post it in a place you will see it regularly.

____

____

____

____

Success & Goal Achievement: Five Steps to Develop Maximum Self-Confidence[5]

1. ## Make the Choice to Believe in Yourself

    Self-confidence is an attitude you can develop over time. It is your responsibility to take charge of your own self-concept and your beliefs.

2. ## Use Positive Self-Talk and Positive Visualizations to Persuade Yourself

    Utilize positive self-talk and positive visualizations with proper training to achieve a higher level of achievement. Proper physical training is not the only factor to be successful. What you think and what you visualize are important factors as well.

3. ## Give Up the Words "I Can't"

    The words "I can't" disempower you; The words you think and say affect your brain and body. Replace these words with "I can" or "I will" if they are in the realm of possibility.

4. ## Ignore What Others Think of You

    If having others believing in you were a requirement for success, most of us would never accomplish anything. Base your decisions about what you want to do on your goals and desires, not the goals or opinions of others. Follow your heart.

5. ## Constantly Acknowledge Your Positive Past

    Most people in our culture remember their failures more than their past. Most people underestimate and underap-

5 Jack Canfield, **https://jackcanfield.com/blog/self-confidence/**

preciate the number of successes they've had, compared to the number of failures they've had. Research has shown that the more you acknowledge your past successes, the more confident you become in taking on and successfully accomplishing new ones.

Exercise:

Choose one of the five criteria above that you want to diligently improve upon:

____

What steps will you take or give a specific example for how you will improve in this area?

The Self-Confidence Cycle

Self-Talk affects Self-Image which affects your Actions/ Behaviors which affects your Results, which then affects your Self Talk. You can help yourself or hurt yourself on this cycle.

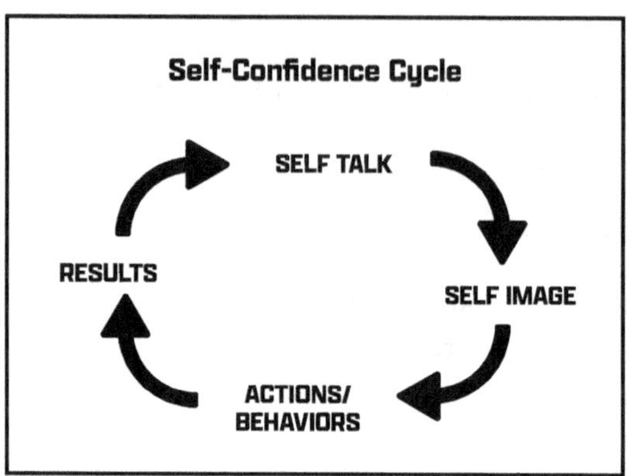

If a person can improve their self-talk and self-image, they will be well on their way to better actions and behaviors. This will likely lead to better performance and improve the chances of better results.

Consequently, start with these two factors: self-talk and self-image. You cannot completely control your self-talk, but you can choose whether to believe your thoughts. Your self-image is even more powerful as to how it affects your attitudes (self-talk), expectations, actions and behaviors, and performances in all areas of your life.

What can you do to allow yourself to have a positive and constructive self-image, and thus a happier and more constructive life?

The Confidence Altitude Check

Are You Afraid of Heights?

Do higher expectations and more success lead you to get nervous and feel uncomfortable?

Do you feel like the air is thinner as you climb the ladder of success, and you start to "choke" in pressure situations?

Do you experience a fear of success, as opposed to a fear of failure, and lose confidence because of the higher expectations?

What suggestions do you have for yourself or a teammate on how to be comfortable with a higher altitude of success?

Confidence Reflections

Two Ways to Deal with a Lack of Confidence (Tennis Mind Game)

1. Dig deep to find and face your fears.
2. Stop thinking about the past and future and become immersed in the now.

Self-reflect, then discuss your thoughts with a teammate or coach.

Go Confidently Toward Your Dreams

We all have dreams. But what improves the chances of dreams coming true is action and confidence. The operative words in this reflection are:

- Confidently
- Direction
- Dreams

What steps do you need to take to go confidently in the direction of your goals?

"Confidence involves risk-taking.
Are you willing to say, 'Yes, I Can!'?"

Ben Loeb, Author

CHAPTER 3

EMOTIONAL MANAGEMENT

Introduction to Emotional Management

The "*What*":

Emotional management is simply that—the managing of your emotions. It is the managing of your thoughts and feelings particularly in stressful situations. It's how you react under stress or in pressure situations.

The "*Why*":

Emotional management is a skill. It is very important to learn how to re-direct your thoughts when your emotions are having a negative effect and you need to regroup. Proper management of your emotions will lead to a better mindset and a better ability to perform.

The "*How*":

Self-awareness of how well you manage your emotions before, during, and after the game are critical to your success and your overall happiness on and off the court. Take a breath to help re-center yourself. Problem-solve on how to be resilient.

The following exercises will give you specific opportunities to improve your emotional management skills.

Break the Chain!

Bear down and break the psychological chain that binds you.

List a psychological obstacle that is holding you back from performing with emotional balance.

____

____

____

What can you do about the obstacle to be psychologically free?

____

____

____

____

Positive Emotion and Thinking Correlation

When we experience **positive emotion**, our thinking expands.

"We literally see more, allowing us to face our problems with clear eyes, make creative connections, and see more possible solutions for problems."

Barbara Frederickson, Ph. D.;
University of Michigan professor, from her book *Positivity*

How do you feel when you play with negative emotions?

How do you feel when you play with positive emotions?

What can you do in the moment to change your emotional state from negative to positive?

Uncomfortable Places

You have to be willing to go to **uncomfortable** places to be **successful**.

Describe the "uncomfortable places" you find yourself in during competition.

What can you do to move from an uncomfortable psychological place to a mindset that is more conducive to success?

The Emotional Markers of Mental Toughness[5]

What is mental toughness? So much of mental toughness is emotional toughness. This exercise focuses on the different elements of emotion that have a direct impact on mental toughness.

Noted sport psychologist James Loehr suggests that mental toughness is "the ability to consistently perform toward the upper range of your talent and skill regardless of competitive circumstances." According to Loehr, mental toughness is not about being mean or cold, but it does involve certain emotional markers.

Evaluate yourself on the four emotional markers listed below. Give yourself a point value for each category and a total score using this grading scale: A = 4 points; B = 3 points; C = 2 points; D = 1 point.

- **Emotional flexibility** - the ability to handle different situations in a balanced or non-defensive manner.
- **Emotional responsiveness** - the ability to stay emotionally engaged in the competitive situation (not withdrawn).
- **Emotional strength** - the ability to sustain your fighting spirit no matter what the circumstances.
- **Emotional resiliency** - the ability to handle setbacks and recover quickly.

Total Score: _____

6 Ben Loeb, *Next Level Coaching*

Once you have your total score, you can determine your Emotional Composite Index (ECI). Calculate your ECI by finding your average score (total score divided by four).

Round off to one decimal point. ECI:________

1. Compare your average score with teammates.
2. Choose an emotional marker to discuss with a teammate or a coach.

Emotional marker chosen: ____________________

1. What can you do to achieve a high score on that emotional marker?

2. Identify another marker for which you have a low score (if applicable) and decide how to improve it.

Build Success through a T.E.A.M.S. Approach

Training my **E**motional **A**gility and **M**ental **S**trength will build personal success![7]

What are you doing to train your...

- **Emotional agility** - your *ability to adapt* to changes in your environment (i.e., the game).
- **Mental strength** - *the resolve you have* when you face challenges.

Which "team" are you on?

Are you with yourself (partner) or do you fight yourself (opponent) when you face adversity?

Response & Plan:

[7] *TEAMS acronym courtesy of Mick Lynch, sport psychologist, Winona State University*

Framing My Emotional Response to Competitive Play

When I compete, I want to feel...

When I face adversity, I will...

Framing My Emotional Response to Competitive Play

Reframe Stress

What are the stressors in your performance arena?

How do you respond to stress?

How do you best recover from different types of stress?

How can you reframe stress to be more in alignment with your purpose and values?

Emotional Recovery Coping Choices for a Better Life

Select three of the ten coping skills listed below that you use or that would be good for you.

HEALTHY RECOVERY COPING CHOICES	
Exercise	Meditating (including focus on breathing)
Getting Out in Nature	Yoga
Reading	Spending time with friends
Writing	Talking to someone you trust
Other	Setting boundaries and saying No

Will you use the coping skills (use a checkmark)

___on a regular basis (lifestyle) or

___under specific conditions (situational)

Game Plan: Write down some specifics about when you will use one or more of your selected coping mechanisms and what you intend to get out of it.

The 3 Rs Sequence for Competitive Play

BEFORE/PAUSE IN COMPETITIVE PLAY		DURING COMPETITIVE PLAY
RESPOND STAGE	**REFOCUS STAGE**	**REINVEST STAGE**
ABCs • **Act: Strong Body Language** • **Re-centering Breath** • **Cue word/phrase/image**	**Re-start** • **Game Plan** • **Rituals** *(pre-action routine)*	**EFT - Energy/Focus/Trust** • **Competitive energy** • **In the moment focus** • **Trust in your technique**

The table above shows the three stages that apply before and during competitive play for sports that involve stop and go action. Some examples of these sports include football, basketball, volleyball, wrestling, tennis, golf, and many others. It's utilized when you have a stop in the action where you have time to respond, then refocus before the next play or point.

There are other sports in which the athlete could utilize just the Refocus Stage, before a basketball free throw, swim race, diving, track & field, or gymnastics event, etc. The refocus stage can be thought of as the preparation stage immediately before the next sport action.

Reflect on how you can use the 3Rs in your sport to improve your on-court/on-field mental performance routine.

What resonates with you on how you can utilize the 3Rs in your sport?

Emotional Management Reflections

The 3 Rs of Composure

R - **Recognize** you are dwelling on mistakes

R - **Regroup** by interrupting the chain of thought

R - **Refocus** on the next play/point

The 3 Rs of Dealing with Defeat

R - **Reflect** - what could you have done better or differently?

R - **Regroup** - what can you do to get to a better place?

R - **Re-energize** - what should you do to get your positive and competitive energy going again?

Respons-ability

Your ability to respond to adversity.

Do your actions meet your ability to respond to a stressful situation?

Do you give into the adversity in your response, or do you rise above it?

CHAPTER 4

FOCUS/
MEDITATION

Introduction to Focus/Meditation

The *"What"*:

Focus is your ability to separate relevant cues from irrelevant cues. Focus is your ability to pay attention to what you can control or influence in the moment. Meditation is the relaxing of your mind, which can help you find a state of calm and quiet.

The *"Why"*:

The ability to focus on relevant cues, in the present moment, will have a direct effect on performance level. Proper focus will help the person find a state of flow where you lose a sense of time and any awareness of consequences. You will likely achieve better results if you focus on the things that create winning, rather than focus on winning itself.

The *"How"*:

Focus on things you can control that will help you be at your best and disregard the rest. Some factors include, attitude, effort, strategy, an inner belief, and your ability to relax under pressure. Start with focusing on your breathing to find the present moment and then ready yourself to perform.

The following exercises will give you specific opportunities to improve your focus skills.

Focus Exercises & Reflective Thinking Questions

Single Point Focus Exercises

Focus on the objective as stated below. When your mind deviates from the objective, re-direct your attention back to the desired focal point. These mindfulness exercises help you to become present-focused and calm, and train you to be able to redirect your attention when you need to.

1. **The Breath** - pay attention to the rhythm and timing of your breathing.
2. **An Object** - for a tennis player, focus your attention on a tennis ball.
3. **An Image** - a circle with a dot in the middle of it. When your attention deviates, then pull the dot back to the center of the circle. This represents being re-centered.

Practice each of the three focus methods above for a minute. Determine which one works best for you for practicing off-the-court/field focus.

Reflective Thinking (AKA Contemplative Questions)

Answer the following questions in the space provided.

1. Why do you play your sport?

2. What do you want to become as a person through playing this sport?

3. How is participation in competitive athletics affecting my self-esteem? Do I need to adjust my perspective because of it?

4. How do I want other people to view me in this competitive arena?

Relaxation Exercises

Progressive Muscle Relaxation - tense and then relax different muscle groups in your body. Utilize your breathing to better feel the relaxation. When you exhale, imagine tension from that particular muscle group leaving your body. Include among the muscle groups: (1) hands and forearms; (2) shoulders; (3) head & neck; (4) upper legs; (5) feet, ankles, lower legs.

Do the exercise above with each muscle group.

Grade yourself on a scale of 1-10 with 1 being low and 10 being a high success rate of feeling the difference between muscle tension and relaxation.

Autosuggestion Training - Use deep breathing in conjunction with repeating an affirmation. An affirmation is a positive thought about yourself. Examples include: I feel calm; I am confident; Calm & Confident; I chose happiness in life; I accept me; I let go of self-defeating habits. Try this for a minute.

What is your affirmation?

Visualization of On-Court/Field Play

Do some deep breathing to allow yourself to get into the zone of calm and quiet.

Then use visual imagery to rehearse dealing with an on-court/on-field scenario.

There are two perspectives you can use: (1) **external** or (2) **internal/kinesthetic**:

- An external perspective is to see yourself performing like you are watching a video.
- An internal/kinesthetic perspective is from the inside of you as you feel the sensations.

Some **scenario examples** are below. Focus on....

1. Warm-up and/or starting a match (managing nerves).
2. Performing the way you want to play—physically, mentally, and emotionally.
3. Overcoming an obstacle like a momentum switch against you; dealing with adversity.
4. Playing with the lead.
5. Playing from behind.
6. Closing out a match.
7. Post-match perspective.

Do some visualization exercises of 3 to 10 minutes on a scenario of your choice. Fill in the table below for your initial visualization sessions. After that either create your own table or do visualization exercises without recording them.

Daily visualization (or at least a few times per week) is recommended for sport or life scenarios.

Date	Duration	Scenario

Freedom from Internal Conflict

"Imagine the experience of being free from all internal conflict." The following is an except on mental toughness written by expert Chris Dorris:

> Spend a moment with that powerful phrase — having no internal conflict. Imagine the experience of being free from all internal conflict.
>
> I equate the term Mental Toughness Training with a heightened consciousness. And I equate the term heightened consciousness with enlightenment. It's all the science of happiness or the game of eliminating internal conflict.
>
> The practice or discipline of self-inquiry is the practice of training yourself to choose to experience reality in a non-problematic way. Imagine seeing no problems. Seeing only situations, opportunities, and beauty.
>
> When I view the world in an inspiring way, I activate dopamine — the on switch for all the brain's learning centers. When I can view the world that way, I am further empowered to creatively solve its "problems"![8]

8 Chris Dorris, **https://christopherdorris.com/conflict-free/**

1. List a sport experience or lie experience where you identify the internal conflict.

2. What is your plan to eliminate the internal conflict or at least manage it the next time you experience it?

The Best Stress Buster

The neuroscience research of **meditation** indicates the practice can rewire key parts of your brain involving self-awareness, compassion, and resilience.

Dan Harris, author of "How to Find Peace Anytime," suggests you begin practicing meditation slowly, devoting five to ten minutes a day. He added that at the start if you find time for one minute a day, you can count that a win. The practice of meditation gets easier the longer you keep at it.[9]

Below are suggestions for a beginning meditation exercise:

Physical Position

Sit comfortably with your spine reasonably straight. Sit cross-legged on the floor or sit in a chair. You may close your eyes or leave them open and adjust your gaze to a neutral point on the ground.

Attention Control

Bring your full attention to the feeling of your breath going in and out. Pick a spot where it's most prominent, such as your belly, your chest, or your nostrils. Instead of thinking about your breath, focus on the physical sensations from the breathing. To maintain focus, make a quiet mental note on each in breath and out breath, like "in" and "out."

Re-Focus

Every time you catch yourself wandering, move your attention back to the breath. As soon as you start to focus on your

9 Dan Harris, Reader's Digest, "How To Find Peace Anytime, Anyplace," June 2020

breath, you'll start having all sorts of random thoughts. This is totally normal. The objective is to notice when you're distracted and begin again... and again.

Next Step in Meditation (Options):

- **Count Your Breaths:** Count your breaths from one to ten, and then start over. Breathing in and then out is one.
- **Recite a Short Phrase:** An example could be "Just this breath." This should help with keeping you present-focused.
- **Recruit an Image:** For instance, imagine the in breath as a gentle wave moving onto the shore (pshhhh), and on the out breath, the wave recedes, (sssshh). Repeat.
- **Guided Audio Meditation:** Find a guided audio meditation session from someone else or create one yourself. Utilize a script that meets your goal.

Focus 101: Ignore Results to Get Them

Most people would agree you need good results to feel successful. But how should you go about getting those results? What is the athlete focusing on during competition? Is it an "outcome" focus or a "process" focus?

An "outcome" focus involved focusing on factors outside of your complete control such as results, rankings, and beating others. A "process" focus involves focusing on what you need to do to perform your best such as preparation, technique, or tactics. The athlete has more control with a process focus.

An outcome focus may actually reduce the chances of achieving the results you want. Two reasons why are (1) If you're focused on the outcome, you aren't focused on the process, namely, what you need to do to perform your best during the competition; (2) What makes you nervous before a competition is typically the outcome, not the process. A fear of losing takes away from your optimal focus in the moment and creates unnecessary stress.

In contrast, when you focus on the process you are focusing on what you need to do to perform your best in that moment. And if you perform well, you're more likely to achieve the result you wanted in the first place. In other words, focus on the things that create winning and not on winning itself.

It is unrealistic to not think about results at all during the competition. Consequently, your challenge is what to do when your mind does fixate on results. First, become aware that you are focusing on the outcome. Then re-focus on your next best move.

Recognize that you can only focus on one thing at a time. Replace your outcome focus with a will to compete and a will to excel in the moment. This shift in thinking is process oriented. Furthermore, remind yourself why you compete beyond to win. This change gets you out of thinking mode and into a feeling mode, generating powerful emotions, such as excitement about the challenge of competing.

Write a personal focus statement on what you will apply from this exercise. My personal focus statement is:

I will focus on...

Relevant vs Irrelevant Cues

"There's more stuff going on inside him than you think, but he's able to siphon out everything he doesn't need and put his energies toward what he does."

Ricky Elliott, caddie for Brooks Koepka,
PGA Tour 5-Time Major Champion

What are some thoughts or feelings you do not need that get in your way?

What type of thoughts or feelings do you need to perform well?

Two Ways of Meditating with Anxiety[10]

Many people turn to meditation to relieve anxiety and stress, to build our capacity for resilience. According to happiness expert and author Narayan Liebenson, "There are, however, two distinct approaches to anxiety in mindfulness meditation. And they lead to different kinds of results." He writes:

Approach #1 (The Anchor)

Meditation helps you calm down. We calm and steady the mind by sustaining the attention on a single "**anchor**" such as the breath, or a phrase or mantra, or the sensations of the body. Doing this brings about a kind of inner peacefulness."

Approach #2 (The Inquiry)

Look at your experience and learn from it. We still cultivate calm and inner silence, but we use this to prepare for **inquiry**. For example, looking directly at anxiety, we begin to see its impermanent and impersonal nature; it is just a temporary experience. We see that anxiety is present because of the want or need to control that which is uncontrollable. This kind of wisdom is what brings lasting peace and inner freedom. Look at anxiety and think of this process as having three steps.

Step 1: Instead of isolating the attention on one object, such as the breathing, we broaden the field of awareness to include whatever is happening in the present moment. *What is being thought? How does it feel?* Recognizing the feeling for what it is *(i.e., this is anxiety)* is a huge leap of consciousness. With this awareness, we can make different choices in

10 Narayan Liebenson, Cambridge Insight Meditation Center, **www.tenpercent.com**

our lives rather than have our actions and thoughts dictated by our past conditioning.

Step 2: The second step is being open to allowing and accepting whatever is coming up. We accept what is, even if it is difficult (as anxiety generally is). We get close to it in order to discern for ourselves what will perpetuate misery and what will bring greater peace.

Step 3: We look at what has been accepted, to see whether it is to be encouraged or let go of. *Is it true? Is this helpful or hurtful*? We cultivate an openness to learn from our experiences. This seeing is known as insight: seeing into how things are, so that we can live in harmony instead of in struggle. Anxiety decreases not because we become better at banishing it once it arises, but because we have learned to coexist with it, to learn from it, and to not be captured by it.

How can you use either "the anchor" or "the inquiry" mediation approach to become better at dealing with anxiety, or other emotions you may struggle with, on or off the field of play?

Breathing Exercise Techniques and Visualization[11]

"Practicing a regular, mindful breathing exercise can be calming and energizing and can even help with stress-related health problems"

Andrew Weil, M.D.

Below are two breathing exercises to reduce stress. These breathing exercises are something you can control and regulate. Breathing is a useful tool for achieving a relaxed and clear state of mind. Athletes may find either of these two breathing exercises beneficial as recommended by wellness expert Dr. Andrew Weil:

- **The 4-7-8 Breathing Exercise (also called the Relaxing Breath)**
- **Breath Counting**

Dr. Weill writes:

Try both breathing exercises and techniques and see how they affect your stress and anxiety levels.

The 4-7-8 Breathing Exercise (Relaxing Breath)

Although you can do the exercise in any position, sit with your back straight while learning the exercise. Exhale completely through your mouth, making a whoosh sound.

11 Dr. Andrew Weil, **https://www.drweil.com/health-wellness/body-mind-spirit/stress-anxiety/breathing-three-exercises/**

- Close your mouth and inhale quietly through your nose to a mental count of four.

- Hold your breath for a count of seven.

- Exhale completely through your mouth, making a whoosh sound to a count of eight.

- This is one breath. Now inhale again and repeat the cycle three more times for a total of four breaths. Do this exercise at least twice a day. (If the 4-7-8 method feels too long, try 4-1-5.)

Use it whenever anything upsetting happens—before you react. Use it whenever you are aware of internal tension or stress in athletics or in other facets of your life.

Breath Counting

This is a simple breathing technique much used in Zen practice. Sit in a comfortable position with the back straight. Close your eyes and take a few deep breaths. Then let the breath come naturally without trying to influence it

- To begin the exercise, count "one" to yourself as you exhale.

- The next time you exhale, count "two," and so on up to "five."

- Then begin a new cycle, counting "one" on the next exhalation.

- Never count higher than "five," and count only when you exhale. Try to do this for 5 to 10 minutes of this form of meditation.

Post-Meditation Breathing

Do some visualization training, seeing yourself performing the way you want to perform physically, mentally, and emotionally. You can also visualize how you will perform when you face adversity.

Guided Breathing Exercise

The following breathing exercise comes from sports performance experts Mind Ready.[12] They write:

1. **Find a comfortable seated position** with your feet planted on the ground and your back straight. You can close your eyes or keep them open, whichever you prefer.

2. **Begin by taking a few deep breaths** in through your nose and out through your mouth. As you inhale, focus on expanding your belly. As you exhale, focus on releasing any tension or stress in your body.

3. Once you have settled into a rhythm of deep, slow breaths, **bring your attention to your breath.** Notice the sensation of the air flowing in and out of your body.

4. As you continue to breathe deeply and slowly, try **counting each inhale and exhale.** You can count "one" on the inhale, and "two" on the exhale. Continue to count to ten and then start over again, focusing solely on your breath and the counting.

5. If your mind starts to wander, gently **redirect your attention back to your breath** and the counting. Try not to get frustrated with yourself if this happens - it is natural for the mind to wander during meditation. Simply acknowledge the thoughts and let them pass, returning your focus to your breath.

12 https://www.linkedin.com/posts/mindready_sport-psychology-coaching-for-athletes-activity-7027324507023450115-YA8e/

Duration: Start with 1 minute then work your way up to 3 minutes, then 5-10 minutes.

Goal: The guided breathing exercise helps you to feel more relaxed and centered.

Note: You can add on a visualization component after the meditative breathing (optional)

Date	Time Duration (minutes)	Grade (5=high; 1=low)

The Morning Breathing Ritual

1. Breathe naturally and slowly as you count your breaths from 10 down to 1.
2. Feel yourself becoming relaxed as you solely focus on your breathing.
3. Then ask yourself this question: **What do I want to be today?** or **What is my intention for the day?**

Note: This short breathing exercise can also be done at any time or in preparation before an important event.

Focus Reflections

"The difference between winning and losing in a competitive match-up is who wins the big moments. How do you win the big moments?

- Embrace the challenge of the situation
- Become present-focused on the task
- Attack it with conviction.

"Make 'Win the Moment' a motto that goes beyond the outcome. It reflects on the mindset needed to bring out your best now."

Ben Loeb, author

"Reactions = Holding on to the past. Responses = Choosing a new step forward in the present. Keep your responses greater than your reactions."

Zach Brandon, mental performance coordinator,
Arizona Diamondbacks

"I just went pitch, pitch, pitch, pitch, rather than pitch, breath, take a breath, relax, and then pitch. But I just tried to go after them as best I could. Ultimately, I've got to take a reset every now and then."

Drew Rom, pitcher, St. Louis Cardinals

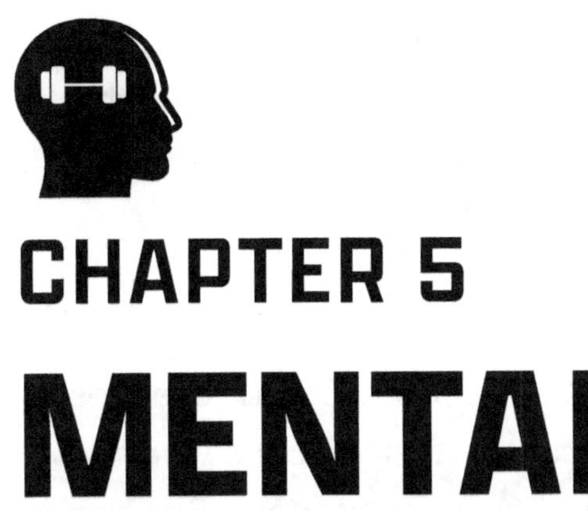

CHAPTER 5

MENTAL TOUGHNESS

Introduction to Mental Toughness

The "*What*":

Mental toughness is the ability to deal with challenges in pressure situations. Mental toughness has both a mental and an emotional component to it. It involves your mental strength (i.e., focus on relevant cues) and your emotional strength (i.e., resiliency). Mental toughness is affected by how well you respond to the resistance from others.

The "*Why*":

Mental toughness is essential to improve your chances of winning when you face difficult obstacles from a worthy foe. Physical and mental preparation are important. But it's the mental/emotional skill set you have in crunch time against formidable resistance that will often determine the outcome.

The "*How*":

Mental toughness skills come in part from your natural mental make-up and your outlook on sport and life. But it is also affected by your experience in tough situations and from a firm belief in your ability to handle adversity. Visualize yourself being mentally tough and then act like it when you need it most.

The following exercises will give you specific opportunities to improve your mental toughness skills.

What Is Mental Toughness?

Author David L Rockwood, in his book *Closing the Gap: Applied Sport Psychology for High School*, writes:

> Mental Toughness is the ability to bounce back quickly and constructively **from setbacks.** The truth of the matter is that everyone is affected by setbacks, but when unexpected things happen the mentally tough athlete is able to rebound quickly and fight all the harder.

> Mental toughness is **refusing to not give up no matter what.** Whether winning or losing, on good days or bad days, healthy or injured, the tough athlete never gives up.

> Mental toughness is the ability to **stay emotionally alive, engaged and connected** under pressure.

On a scale of 1 (low) to 10 (high), how mentally tough are you? What is your reasoning for your score?

What advice would you give on how to be mentally tough?

The T.A.C.C. Mindset Target[13]

1. Review the TACC illustration plus the comparative stages of energy.
2. Decide which stage you typically play in when it matters most (crunch time).
3. What advice would you give to yourself or to another athlete on how to compete in the challenge stage?

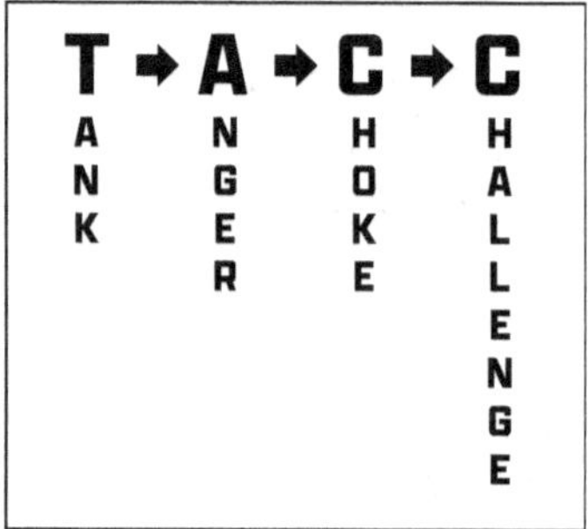

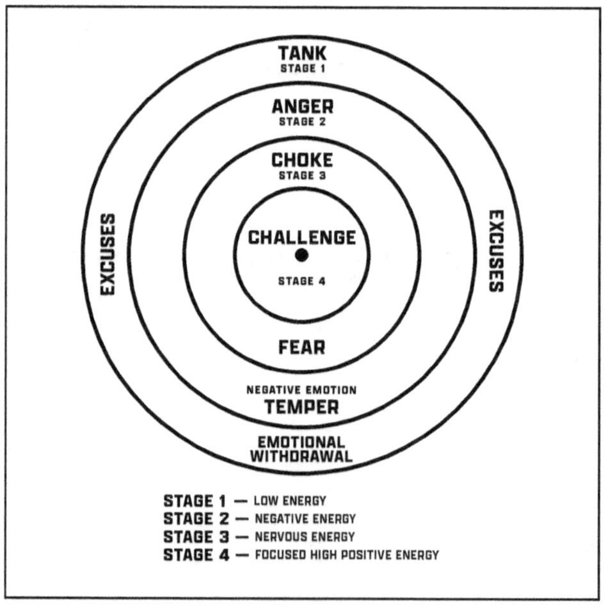

13 https://ushsta.org/the-ideal-performance-state/

Emotional Balance

Emotional Balance = Emotional Control + Competitive Fight

Emotional Balance - A Must! In competitive athletics you need to manage your emotions and at the same time have a fighting spirit. You need to have a mixture of poise (emotional control) and a competitive spirit (competitive fight). You need to know which you need more of depending on the ebbs and flowsof the competition. Engage in the challenge before you with conviction and a mindset to be a problem solver.

Visualize balancing yourself on the tightrope no matter what comes your way.

Describe what it will take for you to play with emotional balance.

Tom Brady's Mental Toughness:
4 Principles He Relied On[14]

Legendary NFL quarterback Tom Brady was known for advocating how important thoughts, emotions, and attitudes are when working to achieve peak performance—especially in facing a challenge or adversity. On his website, the TB12 team wrote:

> Staying positive and determined when things don't go as planned is a critical component of Tom Brady's mental toughness. Here are four keys to Tom Brady's mental toughness that you can apply in your own life.
>
> **#1 START EACH DAY WITH A POSITIVE OUTLOOK**
>
> If you don't believe in yourself, why is anyone else going to believe in you?
>
> **#2 FOCUS ON GIVING YOUR BEST EFFORT**
>
> Tom likes to spend his day focusing on giving his best possible effort toward what he wants to achieve. He applies this simple tactic during games. His experience is that pursuing maximum effort leads to a lasting brand of satisfaction, regardless of the results.
>
> **#3 WHEN SOMETHING DOESN'T GO YOUR WAY, CHOOSE TO STAY POSITIVE**
>
> It's essential to know the difference between the things you can control and the things you can't. You may not have control over what happens, but you can choose how you react.

14 **https://tb12sports.com/blogs/tb12/tom-bradys-mental-toughness**

#4 LEARN FROM LOSSES

Rather than go into a dark place when things don't work out, or if you have a bad day, make a different choice, Tom advises. "Whenever my team loses a game, it's an opportunity to learn something. If we've lost but I've learned something, the game turns into a positive experiment."

Put a checkmark by one of the four principles above, and then elaborate below on how you will incorporate that principle into your life or on the field of play.

What Matters Most Is How You See Yourself

From a young age we develop an image of ourselves. We see the physical self and the psychological self. Both change over time. For many people, the psychological self can be hard to change if we received negative messages at a young age from others or from ourselves. But you can re-write the script. In competitive athletics, there are highs and lows and not much in between. Winning and losing can have a profound effect on our self-image. It's within your control to decide how you see yourself.

How do you see yourself in a selected area of your life (i.e., competitive athletics)? Consider your thoughts and feelings about yourself in your response.

Is there a need to re-write your own script? If so, how? If not, what do you like about your self-image?

How to Resist Taking Things Personally[15]

Four Reminders to Avoid Taking Things Personally:

#1

Sometimes people project their own insecurities and flaws onto others.

Don't take on their baggage. Realize how they project themselves may say more about how they see themselves than how they see you.

#2

Other people's opinions about you are not a reflection of your worth.

There will probably be someone or some people that may not see you as favorably as you would like. Do not allow what other people may think of you define how you see yourself.

#3

Don't take criticism from someone who may have a different agenda than you.

Other people's opinions have other people's energy.

Understand your purpose for why you are doing what you do.

Then be honest with yourself about your true intentions.

Stay in alignment on a noble path.

15 Source unknown

#4

It's impossible to be perfect.

We will all make mistakes, no matter how hard we try not to.

Instead of beating yourself up over your past, refocus your energy on making amends and changing harmful behaviors.

Summation Statements:
1. Don't take on other people's insecurities.
2. What other people think of you isn't truly who you are.
3. Stay in alignment with your own truth about yourself.
4. Instead of beating yourself up over past mistakes, make amends and change harmful behaviors.

List one action step you will take after reading these statements:

Mental Toughness Suggestions

Before the Competition

- Expect Adversity
- Acknowledge your Triggers
- Visualize your Emotional Response

During the Competition

- Focus on the Controllables
- Replace Negative Self-Ta!k with Encouragement
- Stay Present-Focused

After the Competition

- Evaluate then Celebrate or Be Resilient.
- Find Self-Acceptance No Matter the Result
- Commit to Your Next Step to be ready next time.

Put a check mark next to the one in each category that resonates the most with you.

Mental Toughness Reflections

"When things don't go as planned, that's when you find out what you're made of. Everybody can plan for the game to go the way you expect it to go. Everybody can plan for that. But can you be ready when things don't go that way? When you're in trouble? When you can't find a certain pitch? When you've got to make an adjustment here, battle through some adversity—that's when you find out about yourself."

Jack Flaherty, former pitcher, St. Louis Cardinals

"I just loved seeing our guys compete. I love how they respond in between those four lines. There were some moments of truth there at the end, and probably the bottom line is they won those moments of truth."

Erik Spoelstra, head coach, Miami Heat

"Handle Hard Better"[16]

A meaningful pursuit in life will not be easy. Make yourself a person who handles hard well. Develop your own mental toughness.

Kara Lawson, Duke University Women's Basketball Coach

Tiger Woods' Tips for Handling Pressure

Refuse to yield to pressure—it's the most fun part of being a competitor.

Handle pressure by staying in your natural rhythm and routine. Focus on what you need to accomplish.

Learn from your experiences both positive and negative.

Play with confidence, an assuredness in one's ability to accomplish a task even under the most stressful circumstances.

16 https://www.espn.com/video/clip/_/id/39743241

CHAPTER 6

MENTAL EXCELLENCE

Introduction to Mental Excellence

The "*What*":

Mental excellence involves dealing with the resistance of others, but it is more about bringing out the best in yourself, no matter the ability level of others. It is about finding the mental strength to perform your best relative to your capability, and not as much relative to someone else. Mental excellence is about discovering the best version of yourself.

The "*Why*":

Mental excellence is important because it is "you" centered. It's all about you finding the mental skills within you to excel. You seek a standard of finding your level of personal excellence, no matter the level of your opponent. Mental Excellence is important to become your very best.

The "*How*":

You realize mental excellence is more within your control than mental toughness. This is because it's "you-centered," rather than relative to an opponent. You strive to be your best no matter what. Set realistic yet challenging goals, and then be disciplined in your approach to achieve them.

The following exercises will give you specific opportunities to improve your mental excellence.

Arrivers or Strivers?

I have encouraged the teams I coach to bring out the best in themselves mentally, physically, and emotionally on a regular basis. *Are we willing to choose the path of striving for personal excellence or a path of being satisfied with winning, no matter the level of competition?* One time an athlete responded, "We are going to win the state championship either way."

That response was indicative of an attitude that supports doing only what it takes to be good enough to win and nothing more. In short, this athlete was an *arriver*. An arriver is an athlete who wants to be good enough to win, but not good enough to maximize their true potential.

A *striver* is an athlete who seeks to bring out the very best in themselves. They want to discover their true potential. They will train hard and do the right things to win and to find their best self.

Ask yourself as a player, as a coach, or as a team, "What is the athlete's and the team's attitude toward achievement? What defines success?" Jeff Moore of Moore Leadership suggests the athlete, or the team, ask, "Are we arrivers or strivers? Are we driven to be winners or champions?" The following table illustrates the characteristics of both.

ARRIVER'S (WINNERS)	STRIVER'S (CHAMPIONS)
Results-Driven	**Process-Driven**
Driven to compare favorably with others	Driven to compete to a standard of excellence
More interested in their **reputation**	More interested in their **character**
Motivated to move from what is to a specific desired **result**	Motivated to move from what is to **what could be**
Primarily motivated by **external rewards**	Primarily **self-motivated**
Winners make decisions after asking **"How will this make us look?"**	Champions make decisions after asking **"Does this support who we are?"**
Winning teams are driven **to compare favorably** to another team	Champion teams have a **strive together** spirit
Winning teams are built from the **outside-in** (compare to others)	Championship teams are built from the **inside-out** (push each other to compare beyond any comparative measure)

Do you consider yourself a striver? Why? And if you are not a striver, explain what steps you need to take to become one.

1. Discuss your self-evaluation with teammates.
2. Is your team more oriented toward being winners or champions?
3. Write down one to three steps you can take as a team and/or as an individual to be a striver with a champion attitude.

Standards of Excellence

Above the line behaviors:
1. High intention for the group
2. Competitive/Cooperative direction
3. Show respect for teammates and coaches
4. Engaged in the process
5. Primarily team-oriented.

Below the line behaviors:
1. Self-centered intention within the group
2. Resistant to direction/decisions
3. Lack respect for certain teammates or coaches
4. Autopilot during the process
5. Primarily individually oriented

Examples of above the line behaviors:
1. **Accountability** for behavior and reactions to adversity, effort, and results
2. **Responsibility** for being on time and for being considered a "team player."
3. **Communication** in a proper and timely way.

Accountability, Responsibility, and Communication will reveal a lot about your character and how much you value the team.

List some **"Above the Line" behaviors** that you exemplify on a regular basis:

Self-Discipline Is the Key to Success

There are two reasons people are not more successful in their life: First, they don't know how to be successful. Second, even if a person knows what they need to do, it doesn't mean they will. Consequently, the second reason is some people have a resistance to action.

The bottom line is, don't kid yourself or others about who you are or what can be done. Work hard at developing the discipline of reflection and then put it to work.

What area of your sport-life or non-sport life will you take action to show more self-discipline? What action will you take?

The Success Equation

SUCCESS = Ability + Preparation + Effort + Will

Which of the 4 components are within your control (list all that apply)?

What does "Will" mean to you?

What are you willing to do to be achieve "success" as defined above?

Excellence = Motivation x Confidence^2 (E=MC^2)

Motivation – your reason (winning; thrill of competition)

Confidence – what you **think** and how you **feel** about your ability to perform well.

> **Think** – words (self-talk) and pictures (visualize)
>
> **Feel** – emotions (anxiety or joy, threat or challenge) as related to a current situation.

Evaluate your level of motivation and confidence.

Motivation (circle the # that applies to you for how motivated are you to achieve personal excellence?

1	2	3	4	5	6	7	8	9	10
Low									High

Confidence (circle the # that applies to you for how confident are you to achieve personal excellence?

1	2	3	4	5	6	7	8	9	10
Low									High

What words do you use (self-talk) to help your confidence?

What feelings do you have toward competition? Circle the terms that best describes you.

Nervous	Doubtful	Fearful	Self-Image	Threatened
Excited	Psychologically Free	Challenge-seeker	Joyful/Fun	

Five "Must Dos" for Competitive Success[17]

Coaching expert Dr. Jim Taylor writes about competitive success—in particular for ski-racing but his lessons can apply to any sport. I've included a question after each of his "Must-do" suggestions:

Must-do #1: Control or Not to Control

The next time you find that you are under stress, ask yourself one question: "Is the thing that I am worried about under my control?" If it's not, let it go and focus on things you can control.

Q: List some things that are within your control:

Must-do #2: Trust Your Ability on Game Day

There is a time and a place to think about technique: during training. With repetition in training, the technique should become automatic, which is what you want. Whatever capabilities you bring to the game, trust yourself, and go with it on that day.

Q: What are some words or phrases that describe what trusting yourself means to you?

17 https://www.drjimtaylor.com/4.0/5-must-dos-for-race-day-success/

Must-do #3: Pre-Match/Game Preparation

Get physically ready though stretching and warm-up exercises and sport-specific routines. Get mentally prepared through narrowing your focus onto the upcoming game, mentally rehearsing key parts of the game, thinking positively, and actively moving toward your ideal intensity.

Q: Describe your pre-match/game routine:

Must-do #4: Commit Yourself to Your Game Plan

Should you play aggressively or tentatively? Playing cautious against good competition is usually a recipe for disappointment and regret. I like to say, "play smart-aggressive." Commit to play with conviction and a belief in your abilities.

Q: Describe how you want to play in your sport:

Must-do #5: Avoid One Emotion and One Question

After your game, season, career, and life, the statement you want to be able to make is "I gave it everything I had." And the emotion you want to experience is pride in knowing that you left it all out there.

Q: What do you take pride in, win, or lose, in your competitive arena?

The Mental Edge – Ben Askren[18]

Two-time NCAA men's wrestling champion Ben Askren has written about three factors he attributes to success:

1. Hard Work
2. Open to Learning
3. Love a Challenge/Not Afraid to Lose

Evaluate yourself on each factor using the scale below:

Hard Work (sustained effort)

1	2	3	4	5	6	7	8	9	10
Low									High

Open to Learning (coachable)

1	2	3	4	5	6	7	8	9	10
Low									High

Explain why you think you are coachable (if applicable).

Threat or Challenge

1	2	3	4	5	6	7	8	9	10
Low									High
Afraid to Lose									Love a Challenge

18 Add Source: Ben Askren (2-time NCAA Wrestling Champion) on the Mental Edge 4/17/21

The Mental Excellence Color Scheme

Coaching expert Dr. Jim Loehr developed a mental excellence exercise based on a color scheme.

Different colors represent different characteristics for the emotions an athlete feels during competition. Your emotional state is an indicator of your ability to compete at the upper level of achieving personal excellence. Your "color state" may ebb and flow during competition. It is the athlete's mission to re-calibrate their emotional state to perform in the right color zone for mental excellence.

Color	Red	Black	Light Blue	Deep Vibrant Blue
Characteristics	High Negative Energy	Low Negative Energy	Low Positive Energy	High Positive Energy
	Fearful; Angry	Disinterested; Annoyed	Tired; Weary	Alert; Energetic
	Tight Muscles; Accelerated Mental State; Tunnel Vision	Low-Moderate Muscle Tension; Calmness varies; Unfocused	Relaxed Muscles; Calm Mental State; Unfocused	Relaxed Muscles; Calm Mental State; Focused
	Moderate-Poor Performance #2	Poor-Very Poor Performance #4	Poor Performance #3	Peak Performance #1 ranking

Which color scheme do you typically perform in under pressure situations?

What strategy could you use to find your way back to Deep, Vibrant Blue to achieve your best mental/emotional state for personal excellence?

Mental Excellence Reflections

"In the heat of a moment, sometimes you want to use that energy to lift yourself up, and sometimes you just want to kind of cocoon yourself and really isolate the noise, and focus on breathing and focus on staying present, and focusing on the next point. So, it's really adapting to whatever circumstances have for you and whatever is required in that moment for you."

Novak Djokovic, 24-time Grand Slam Tennis Singles champion

"Take time to think about how you will show up today."

Anonymous

"When two athletes have the same level of ability, the one with the better mindset will win every time."

Dr. Carrie Hastings, team psychologist, LA Rams

CHAPTER 7

MINDFULNESS

Introduction to Mindfulness

The "*What*":

Mindfulness is the conscious awareness of the present moment while calmly accepting one's thoughts and feelings.

The "*Why*":

Mindfulness is important because it allows you to self-regulate overthinking in the moment. It also allows you to become aware ("mindful") of things that are counter-productive to being successful (i.e., dwelling on a past mistake). What are you "mindful" of? And is that helping or hurting you?

The "*How*":

Awareness – practice being aware of what thoughts and feelings you are experiencing. Discover whether these thoughts and feelings are focused on the past, in the present, or on a potential future concern. Let negative emotion or nervous feelings pass, and replace it with a thought that can help you now.

The following exercises will give you specific opportunities to learn more about mindfulness and how it can help you.

Mind Full or Mindful?

Mindfulness allows you to "pay attention to the present moment, on purpose, without judgment" says expert Jon Kabat Zinn.

List an example of how you can become more mindful in an aspect of your life:

The Three A's: The Mindfulness Solution

Here's a helpful practice from Drs. Kristine Eiring and Colleen Hathaway, authors of *Mindfulness and Sport Psychology for Athletes*, called "The Three As":

1. **AWARENESS** - Be *aware* of what is happening (mindfulness).
2. **ACCEPTANCE** - *Accept* what is happening. Don't argue about it in your head.
3. **ACTION** - leave positive and negative thinking, or judgment, out of it. How? Engage in neutral thinking by giving your mind an action step. Become task focused.

The Mindfulness Solution is a quick and easy strategic approach to becoming more mindful of your thoughts—and then what you can do with those thoughts when they are counterproductive.

Think of an example in your performance arena where your thoughts get in the way of you being productive in that moment:

What are you aware is happening?

What do you have to accept about the situation?

What action step do you need to take to get to a better place?

Self-Love Quotes

Competitive athletics, and life itself, can have its challenges. It's hard enough to beat a worthy opponent. It becomes more difficult if you face another opponent from within. Consequently, you need yourself on your side. Self-love is an integral part of staying connected within yourself to better the chances of being successful in your personal pursuits. Reflect on the quotes below and how they impact your life.

1. "I think the reward for conformity is that everyone likes you except yourself."

    Rita Mae Brown

2. "The only person who can pull me down is myself, and I'm not going to let myself pull me down anymore."

    C. JoyBell C.

3. "When a woman becomes her own best friend, life is easier."

    Diane Von Furstenberg

4. "The most terrifying thing is to accept oneself completely."

    C.G. Jung

5. "How you love yourself is how you teach others to love you."

    Rupi Kaur

6. "How would your life be different if...You stopped allowing other people to dilute or poison your day with their words or opinions? Let today be the day... You stand strong in the truth of your beauty and journey through your day without attachment to the validation of others"

Steve Maraboli

7. "Whenever I am in a difficult situation where there seems to be no way out, I think about all the times I have been in such situations and say to myself, "I did it before, so I can do it again."

Idowu Koyenikan

Which quote among these is your favorite?

Explain below how it relates to your life:

Tips for Finding Flow and Self-Awareness Practices

Simple Tips for a Flow Experience

Physical

Find a relaxed tempo; trust your natural rhythm and timing.

Mental

Focus on competing in the moment (present-focused mentality).

Emotional

Be fully engaged in the game with positive energy and no regard for consequences.

Self-Awareness Practices[19]:

Three simple points to remember …

- **Embrace challenges** (because excuses distract).
- **Choose truth** (because drama drains).
- **Create solutions** (because complaints bore).

19 Inspire.com

Create a Winning Mindset Identity

Steps to creating your own personal identity pathway:

Step 1: Self-Talk

Reflect on your own self-talk. What are you saying to yourself in critical situations?

Step 2: Mental Skills

Identify the mental skills you need to be cohesive and connected within yourself.

Some examples include confidence; focus; mental toughness; motivation; fear of failure; fear of success; perfectionism; mindfulness; resilience; energy management; positivity/optimism; mental relaxation; competitiveness; leadership; team-oriented; character & responsibility

List one to three mental skills you need for a winning mindset.

Step 3: Choose Words

Identify one to three words that will become the foundation of your desired identity. Examples of words to choose from (not inclusive of all options): Desire; Focus; Accountability; Adaptability; Resilience; Composure; Belief; Curiosity. Decisiveness; Appreciation; Commitment; Drive; Passion; Pressure; Heart; Coachable

Foundational Words:

Step 4: Ongoing Self-Reflection

Educate yourself daily by setting an intention for the day to remind yourself of the identity you have chosen. The most challenging part is to be brave in living your chosen words in crucial moments.

Should Fun Be Part of the Process or Just the Result?[20]

Everyone loves to win. Winning beats the alternative by a long shot. Have you ever seen the team that comes second dog-pile in the middle of the diamond or on the basketball court? Of course not. Winning is certainly the goal for athletes in competitive athletics.

Should having fun be part of the process toward seeking the outcome of winning? Or does having fun get in the way of winning? Does having fun take away your focus from the task at hand?

Benefits of having fun while competing include:

Psychological Benefits

1. Reduces distractions and puts you in a positive frame of mind.
2. Builds confidence
3. Increases motivation
4. Keeps you focused in the present and prevents overthinking

Emotional Benefits

1. Generates positive emotions, such as joy, excitement, and inspiration.
2. Counters negative emotions such as fear, worry, and despair.

20 Excerpts from Dr. Jim Taylor's "Prime Sport Alert!" Newsletter" (Nov 2019)

Physical Benefits

1. Reduces stress
2. Muscle relaxation
3. Slows your heart rate

Forces that Counter Fun

1. Disappointing results or your self-esteem being tied to your results
2. Slow progress
3. High pressure parents or coaches
4. A "winning is everything" sports culture

Striving to achieve your best and striving to win at the highest level is not always fun. The chase for excellence and the chase to win can be psychologically wearing, emotionally difficult, and physically grinding. There is a price you pay to be highly successful. Consequently, use fun in a conscious and proactive way to better enjoy the process and to put things in perspective.

By creating an "NFL" approach—"No Fun League"—you create a pressure inside you that becomes counter-productive to being composed in the clutch. Have fun in a conscious way by reminding yourself to simply have fun playing the game. See the experience as an opportunity to test yourself mentally, physically, and emotionally, without the results defining you.

Consequently, let fun be part of the process. It will likely lead to more winning rather than less.

Identify ways you can let fun be part of your competitive sport experience.

Mindfulness Scripts

Mindfulness Script #1 Breath Awareness

For the next couple minutes give yourself permission to bring all of your attention to the present moment. You can either close your eyes or find a specific place on the ground to focus your eyes. Now move your attention to your breath... [pause] Notice the sensations of the breath moving in and out of your body. [pause] There is no need to control your breath or breathe in any particular way... simply notice how you are already breathing. [long pause]

When you notice your mind wandering, give yourself permission to recommit your attention to the breath... in this moment. [pause] Notice the sensations of the in breath... and the out breath. [pause] Follow the full cycle of your breath. Notice the inhalation moving through the nose, and throat, down into the chest, and then the belly rising above toward the end of the breath. And with the exhalation, feeling the belly fall back toward your spine, the breath moving out of your lungs, and back out of your throat and nose. Take the next few breaths to follow the full cycle of your breath. [long pause] Take another 2 or 3 breaths and then when you are ready you can open your eyes.

Mindfulness Script #2 Body Scan

Take the next few minutes to settle into the present moment. Preferably close your eyes to make it easier to let go of visual distractions and to focus inwardly. If you prefer not to close your eyes, simply find a spot on the floor or elsewhere to rest your gaze. Focus your attention inwardly, noticing what it physically feels like to be in your body in this moment. [pause]

Notice the overall experience of sensations. Is there tension or relaxation, tightness or ease? [pause] What is your energy like? Are you experiencing an ideal amount of energy, feeling keyed up, or fatigued? [pause] And now, shift your attention to noticing mood. What emotions are present in this moment? Happiness, sadness, upset, anxiousness, frustration, excitement, or feeling neutral... and where do you notice this in your body? [long pause]

Now turn your attention to the state of your mind. Is there a buzz of energy in the mind, or a whirlwind of thoughts, calm, or tranquility? [pause] Offer acceptance to each thought, emotion, and sensation that arises. [long pause] Take the next few moments to notice what it is like to be inside your body. When you are ready you can open your eyes or leave your focal point.

Exercise:

Record either or both mind scripts or have a someone (i.e., a coach, parent, etc.) recite one of them to you to practice mindfulness training.

Mindfulness Reflections

Don't think too much.

You'll create a problem that wasn't even there in the first place.

Mental Skills Awareness

"Between stimulus and response there is space.
In that space there is our power to choose our response.
In our response lies our growth and freedom."

Viktor E. Frankel, author, Man's Search for Meaning

Learning to Breathe

"Breathing is something I've been working on the last couple of months with my psychologist. I find breathing very important especially when I'm performing or playing. Breathing helps me control myself and have full control of what I'm doing out there."

Stefanos Tsitipas, champion, 1000 Professional Tennis Title

CHAPTER 8
MOTIVATION

Introduction to Motivation

The "*What*":

Motivation is the "motive," or the *why* a person is driven to reach a goal. Motivation is reflected in a person's level of dedication, and their inner will to achieve that goal. It is the fuel that drives you if you have the desire to succeed.

The "*Why*":

Motivation is a critical element of achieving personal excellence. You must be motivated if you want to reach challenging goals. Internal motivation (i.e., from within you), such as internal gratification of accomplishment, is generally considered more of a driving force than external motivation (i.e., from an outside source), such as recognition. Determine what is your internal driving force.

The "*How*":

Determine what motives you, or the "why" you do what you do. When your motivation level slips, remind yourself of what motivates you to sustain the drive to do it. Set goals that you want to achieve. Then create a plan or steps you need to take to achieve it. Then the hard part: Take action and stick to it.

The following exercises will give you specific opportunities to learn more about what could motivate you and what has motivated others.

Motivation

"This is a team of crazy competitors and it might sound cliche, but I have never been a part of a group that **loves competing** like we do.

"Now that we're finally here, we're not taking no for an answer. We're competing for each other, playing hard. We've always been doing that but now it's a lot more heightened because we have the attention of the nation and the volleyball world now, which makes it a lot more fun."

Madison Lilley, volleyball player, Kentucky Wildcats
Women's Volleyball, 2021 National Champions

What do you take from this? How does this inspire you?

Five Great Motivational Quotes

1. We are what we repeatedly do. Excellence, therefore, is not an act but a habit.

Aristotle

2. The best way out is always through.

Robert Frost

3. Do not wait to strike till the iron is hot; but make it hot by striking.

William B. Sprague

4. Great spirits have always encountered violent opposition from mediocre minds.

Albert Einstein

5. Whether you think you can or think you can't, you're right.

Henry Ford

Select one of the quotes and comment on how you can use it in your life:

Success-Orientation

The athlete that derives great satisfaction from pursuing success without worrying about the possibility of failure is success-oriented.

For many athletes it is a difficult proposition to not worry about failure especially during crunch time or when the outcome is in doubt (fear of failure). Just the same, it is difficult during crunch time for some athletes to be comfortable within themselves while pursuing success (fear of success). The best thing for the athlete to do is these two things:

1. Embrace the unknown!
2. Thrive on being challenged!

**Rate yourself on a scale of 1-10 (low to high; 5 =average)
on your ability to perform without worrying about failure.
Think about why you feel you deserve a certain score. Write
a response, then discuss with a teammate or with a coach.**

Score _____

Victimized by Hope[21]

The folks at The Center for the Empowerment Dynamic write powerfully about motivation:

> The emotion of hope is one of the most important and positive emotions available to human beings in sport and life. When facing difficult times, hope keeps us moving forward. Dreaming and hoping for success can be motivating. When you create a new vision and desired outcome for yourself, hope absolutely can give you energy to generate it. That is the positive side of hope. But you can become "victimized by hope" if you do not take appropriate action.
>
> Consistently placing your attention and thoughts upon a positive future, without taking action, can actually disempower you. This happens because being overly invested in the future distracts and drains your energy from what is

21 https://theempowermentdynamic.com/hope/

yours to do, today. Instead, engage with what is in front of you now. Tell yourself the truth about your current reality—both that which challenges the future you want to create AND what supports you to move forward.

Take responsibility—and transform the energy you spend on hoping and wishing into taking action by taking the steps toward the life you desire to create on and off the field. It is when you become overly attached to the hope alone, without getting into action, that your hope may work against you.

List an action step you will take in the present to turn hope into achievement in the future:

What Is Your Level of Engagement?

Which descriptor below best describes you regarding your overall engagement (i.e., physically, mentally, emotionally) in your sport, activity, or performance arena?[22]

Fully Engaged - This suggests that your energy management skills are excellent. Your level of engagement is sufficient to fully ignite your talent and skill.

Engaged - This suggests that your energy management skills are high, but not sufficient to fully ignite your talent and skill. You must work to expand your level of engagement.

Disengaged - This suggests that significant obstacles stand in the way of fully igniting your talent and skill. To become an extraordinary performer, you must build significantly stronger energy management skills.

Seriously Disengaged - Your level of disengagement not only significantly undermines your ability to fully ignite your talent and skill, but also prompts disengagement in others. When levels of disengagement such as this persist over time, your health, happiness, and productivity can be seriously compromised.

Explain if there is anything you are willing to do to become more engaged if you seek a higher level of engagement:

22 Human Performance Institute, https://www.jjhpi.com/

Golfer Phil Mickelson on Hard Work and Belief

"I've never been driven by exterior things. I've always been intrinsically motivated because I love to compete. I love playing the game. I love having opportunities to play against the best at the highest level. That's what drives me, and I think the belief that I could still do it inspired me to work harder. I just didn't see why it couldn't be done. It just took a little bit more effort."

Phil Mickelson, 2021 PGA Champion at age 50

What can we learn from Phil's great accomplishment?

Reflect on your own life. Take inspiration from Phil Mickelson's accomplishment. List a personal goal, which does not need to be sports-related. Then go after it with a deliberate approach and the enthusiasm of a 50-year-old trying to win the PGA Golf Championship.

Goal:

List at least one step you will take to accomplish this goal.

Finding A Way to Win

I don't care so much about the exact score, or even the level of performance, as I do about the fight.

It has to be a hard fight, because the hard fights are the most satisfying to win.

And to put the emotional kicker on it, the game would go to the last minute with the outcome still uncertain.

And then someone on my team will do something to win it at the end—*he will find a way to win.*

That's the kind of game where your euphoria is greatest, where the celebration is most spontaneous.

When I'm finished with coaching, those are the games that will remain most vivid in my recollection.

And I'll remember the faces of my players, so intent and so unified, who earned that win with their sweat and blood ...

—Bill Parcells, from *Finding A Way to Win*

Describe a time in your life where you found a way to win. It does not have to be in the context of the sports arena. It was a time when you had to dig deep and give your best effort. It was a time when you felt a great sense of accomplishment either as an individual or as part of a team (sports, work, or a club).

Motivation Reflections

Go "FAR" in Life Managing Fear

F – Be **Free** to explore the unknown.

A – **Accept** the Challenge

R – Be **Resilient**

"Nothing great in the world has been accomplished without passion."

Georg Wilhelm Friedich Hegel

Play with Abandon

Unconcerned about the outcome but focused on playing all out.

"A lot of people are afraid of commitment because it means they'll have to say, 'that's the best I can do.' They elect to be average. When you compete, you decide to find out what your real limits are, not just what you think they are."

Pat Summit, former University of Tennessee
Women's Basketball Coach

"Don't get consumed by the comparison game.
'Stay in your lane, bro' and go!"

Ben Loeb, author

CHAPTER 9

SELF-DISCOVERY

Introduction to Self-Discovery

The "*What*":

Self-Discovery involves a person's curiosity to find out more about themselves. In competitive athletics, self-discovery involves taking mental and emotional risks to discover the best version of yourself.

The "*Why*":

A person will become curious about self-discovery to explore what they can achieve. It could be completing a crossword puzzle, performing well at a school play, achieving your very best on an ACT Test, or overcoming fear in competitive athletics. What is it that you want to discover about yourself?

The "*How*":

Self-discovery starts with knowing your personal values and then determining what drives you to achieve a goal. Self-discovery involves putting less emphasis on comparison to others and more emphasis on focusing on you. Ask "what am I curious to discover about myself?"

The following exercises will give you specific opportunities to learn more about self-discovery.

Self-Discovery: What Drives You?

Answer the following questions as they relate to your performance arena. Then review your responses periodically. Edit your responses, if need be, as your perspective may change.

Question #1: Who Am I? (Self-Discovery)

What attributes do you have as a person that you bring into your competitive arena?

(i.e., high/low confidence, resilience, calm, anger, secure/insecure, focused/unfocused, etc.)

Question #2: Why do I do this? (Motivators)

What motivates you to be involved in this competitive arena?

List the factors that motivate you to be doing this sport or endeavor.

Question #3: What do I want to accomplish? (Vision)

Question #4: How will I get there? (Process goals; steps to take toward goal achievement)

These goals and steps to take can be related to physical, mental, or emotional improvement.

Self-Awareness: An Internal Audit

Most people put so much emphasis on how they compare to others, and less emphasis on figuring out themselves. Introspection is a valued tool in the process of becoming aware of who you are and what you want to accomplish in sport and in life. We yearn for coping skills (i.e., breath control to relax) when we feel anxious. But what about also taking an internal look to become more self-aware. Self-awareness is an "inside-out" approach, while utilizing a coping skill is an "outside-in" approach.

Try using the acronym "CLAD" to create better self-awareness. The word "clad" can be defined as to provide a covering or protective coating. Better self-awareness can act as a protective *psychological* covering. You should want to protect yourself psychologically while still holding yourself accountable. Here are the four "selves" that come from the CLAD acronym:

Do you have...

C Self-Compassion
L Self-Love
A Self-Acceptance
D Self-Discovery

Self-Compassion: ______

Are you kind to yourself? What is your self-talk like? How do you feel about yourself?

A self-compassionate person supports themselves when they underperform in life, make mistakes, or don't get the win! They encourage themselves, rather than criticize themselves.

Self-Love: ______

Self-love involves deep caring, support, and appreciation for oneself. You need to have a mindset that you love the person you are, despite your imperfections or desire for improvement. The love for yourself is unconditional. It is not dependent on success. A question to ask yourself is ***do you still love yourself when you have setbacks in sport or in life?***

Self-Acceptance: ______

Self-acceptance involves seeing things about yourself or about a situation for what they are. A person with self-acceptance has the wisdom to know the difference between what they still can change and what they cannot change. You accept things as they are. You choose to stay connected within yourself, yet you also work toward positive changes or outcomes in the future.

Self-Discovery: ______

Once you set the groundwork for the CLA part of CLAD, with self-**c**ompassion, self-**l**ove, and self-**a**cceptance, you can then explore self-**d**iscovery with enthusiasm and conviction. Self-discovery involves having the motivation for achievement in what you value pursuing.

Use the blank space next to each factor and evaluate yourself on a scale of 1 (low) to 5 (high).

Then do some self-reflection or discuss with a teammate or coach, how you can improve in one or more of your lower graded categories.

Sport Performance Assessment

Time Period (week, month, season):

WANTS Performance Goals & Outcome Goals (emphasize Performance Goals; Outcome Goals are optional)	NEEDS Process Goals (action steps) to Achieve the "Wants"
Example: I want a batting average at .330	Example: I need to spend 20 minutes on batting practice 3 times per week in the off-season.
Example: I want to win a state championship	Example: I need to do visualization training (frequency & duration) on dealing with pressure situations.

Triggers/Tendencies vs Solutions

TRIGGERS OR TENDENCIES THAT WORK AGAINST YOU	SOLUTION
Example: When I miss a shot, I dwell on it.	Example: When I miss a shot, I regroup, and I might acknowledge the correction, but I always move on.

Periodically review your "needs" to have a better chance to achieve your "wants."

Review your triggers or tendencies that work against you and what your solution game plan will be.

Why Do I Play[23]

Why do I play competitive sports?

Is it worth the energy it takes to perform well? Sometimes I don't want to, but I do.

Why do I play?

To stay in shape, to improve a skill, to win at a game—all partial reasons, I suppose. The real reason is confirmation—confirmation that I am in control.

I must make a choice—a choice to show myself that I am a self-starter, that I have self-discipline, and that I can accept responsibility.

Sometimes I must make the choice to endure physical discomfort to reach a team goal or a personal goal.

If I truly care, competing is a test of my strength—not just my physical strength, but also my mental and emotional strength. It is a test of my strength to accept myself no matter the outcome. To take the risk of preparing my best and then giving my best on game day and discovering what happens with no guarantees.

Can I win and lose with class? Do I have the emotional resiliency to accept myself when things do not go my way? This can be a challenge of my "will"—of mind over matter, of me against myself.

23 Original source Unknown; revised by Coach Ben Loeb.

Willpower

Do I have the willpower to discover some things about myself? Strangely, but unmistakably, my "will" is tied to self-discipline, self-denial, self-control, and self-acceptance.

Participation in competitive sports helps create feelings of hope, strength, and conviction that I can make a difference in my own life.

Addiction or Choice

An addiction or choice one might ask.

If I "choose," the value remains genuine. I must participate not out of necessity, not out of satisfying someone else, but out of satisfying me.

If I am part of a team, we can enrich each other's lives. I can also enrich my own life. Why do I play competitive sports?

To have fun—yes, that is part of it. Because I have a strong preference for winning over losing? That could be part of it. But I aspire for more than that. I play to be successful in the ultimate challenge.

The contest of me against myself.

List one compelling take away you have from this article:

Personal Values to Live By

Values

Identify three core personal values you want to live by. Examples but not all inclusive include those below. Two blank lines are provided for you to fill in other values. Circle the values that represent your 3 choices.

- Leadership
- Emotional Management
- Mindfulness (present focus)
- Mental Toughness
- Self-confidence (self-belief)
- Self-acceptance
- Self-responsibility
- Self-discipline
- Competitiveness (fighting spirit)
- Commitment (perseverance)
- Character (integrity)
- Gratitude (appreciation)
- Courage (vulnerability & do it anyway)
- Respect (for self & others)
- Fun (joy)
- Team Support

Give an example of how you exemplify each of these values in your life.

#1

#2

#3

What is your level of intention (commitment) on living these values in your sports world?

1	2	3	4	5	6	7	8	9	10
Low									High

Why Play Competitive Sports?

"Sometimes you're just happy playing. Some people, some media, unfortunately, don't understand that it's okay just to play tennis and enjoy it. They always think you have to win everything, it always needs to be a success story, and if it's not, what is the point? Maybe we have to go back and think, 'Why have I started playing tennis?' Because I just like it. It's actually sort of a dream hobby, that became somewhat a job. Some people just don't get that."

-Roger Federer, 20-time Grand Slam Men's Tennis champion

Is it possible to enjoy the sport, have a competitive mindset, and value the outcome? (all at the same time)

__Yes __No

Why or why not?

Keep-Stop-Start Goal Setting

What do you need to do now in your performance arena (i.e., sport) or in your life?

Suggestions: *Make your entries as specific as possible, measurable and with a time frame when applicable.*

In Your Performance Arena

Keep Doing	Stop Doing	Start Doing

In Your Life

Keep Doing	Stop Doing	Start Doing

Share with a teammate, coach, or friend, then hold yourself accountable.

Fear Statements for Reflection

In *Thinking Body, Dancing Mind: Taosports for Extraordinary Performance in Athletics, Business, and Life*, author, athlete, and winning expert Chungliang Al Huang, writes:

Which statements do you agree with?

Mark an "A" for Agree and a *"D"* for Disagree in the blank provided.

Fear of Failure Statements

- ❑ "Adversity leads to inner strength. I am a better athlete because of it."

- ❑ "Many of us are critical and unkind toward ourselves when we experience setbacks."

- ❑ "Expectations with regard to outcomes are setups for failure. Establish strong preferences, instead, and then do everything within your capability and power to bring those preferences to fruition."

Fear of Success Statements

- ❑ "I deserve and am entitled to the very best there is."

- ❑ "I give myself permission to develop my full potential."

- ❑ "You may choose a road that avoids success, with all its pressures; success becomes a frightening entity. But if you turn your back on your talent, you create another pain to contend with: You must grow old constantly wondering how good you could have been."

Discuss your responses with a teammate, coach, or friend.

To what degree do you have a fear of failure or a fear of success or both? Circle the number of your response.

Fear of Failure

0   1   2   3   4   5

None   Low   High

Fear of Success

0   1   2   3   4   5

None   Low   High

Comments:

BEING HARD ON YOURSELF IS A "LOSING GAME"

Dr. Alan Goldberg writes a newsletter on mental toughness.[24] In one installment he writes:

> Putting yourself down when you fail or make mistakes will NOT make you a better athlete. ON THE CONTRARY! Responding to your failings with **frustration** and **self-directed anger** will only tighten you up and ultimately shut your game down. Playing angry in this way will get you performing at a small percentage of your potential.
>
> Instead, you need to learn to respond to yourself the way a good coach would. You have to be able to forgive yourself for your failings and mistakes. You have to learn to treat yourself with patience and kindness whenever you fail, rather than with impatience and meanness. Beating yourself up for your shortcomings will ultimately kill your motivation and joy of the sport and once you lose those two, you're lost!

Evaluation:

Are you hard on yourself when you do not perform well?

(Scale: O = Not at all, I'm my own best friend; 1 = Low; 3 = Moderate level; 5 = Very Hard on Myself); Circle the number of your response

0	1	2	3	4	5
Zero	Low				High

24 https://www.competitivedge.com

Are you hard on yourself when you lose?

(Scale: O = Not at all, I'm my own best friend; 1 = Low; 3 = Moderate level; 5 = Very Hard on Myself); Circle the number of your response

0	1	2	3	4	5
Zero	Low				High

When percent of the time does anger spur a positive response in you?

0%   25%   50%   75%   100%

What do you recommend doing to foster resilience after a frustrating tough loss?

Discuss your responses with a teammate, coach, or friend.

The Power of Story

Dr. Jim Loehr has spoken about the idea of "change your story, change your game." On the power of story, he notes:

The Rules of Storytelling

The Truth

1. Stories must be grounded in the truth.
2. No Exaggerations; No Denial; No Cover up
3. Your story must be consistent with the facts about your game or level of play.

Your Purpose

Be clear about what you want to get out of the competitive experience in addition to winning. Players' stories must take them where they want to go.

Take Action

1. Players' stories must lead them to hope-filled action.
2. If I do these things, I will improve my chances of reaching my goals.
3. You have a private voice (what you tell yourself) and public voice (what you tell others) in your storytelling.
4. What story are you telling others about your game? Is it consistent with what you tell yourself?

Change Your Story. Change Your Game!

Understand the difference between good and bad storytelling.

Good storytelling is grounded in the truth and includes a plan of action.

Bad storytelling is either to protect your ego (i.e., excuses) or it portrays yourself being absorbed in the problem.

Final Thoughts on Storytelling

The stronger you are as a person, the stronger you will be as competitive athlete in any sport.

You must get your story straight! It's based on the truth and acting on a plan.

Question to answer about where your story is taking you:

1. Do you like who you are becoming because of your sport?

2, Who are you becoming because of your sport?

Just Me

A poem by Tom Krause.

From the time I was little, I knew I was great
'cause the people would tell me, "you'll make it – just wait."
But they never did tell me how great I would be
If I ever played someone who was greater than me.

When I'm in the back yard, I'm king with the ball.
To swish all those baskets is no sweat at all.
But all of a sudden there's a man in my face
Who doesn't seem to realize that I'm king of this place.

So the pressure gets to me; I rush with the ball.
My passes to teammates could go through the wall.
My jumpers not falling, my dribbles not sure.
My hand is not steady, my eye is not pure.

The fault is my teammates – they don't understand.
The fault is my coaches – what a terrible plan.
The fault is the call by that blind referee.
But the fault is not mine; I'm the greatest, you see.

Then finally it hit me when I started to see
That the face in the mirror looked exactly like me.
It wasn't my teammates who were dropping the ball,
And it wasn't my coach shooting bricks at the wall.

That face in the mirror that was always so great
Had some room for improvement instead of just hate.
So I stopped blaming others and I started to grow.
My play got much better and it started to show.

And all of my teammates didn't seem quite so bad.
I learned to depend on the good friends I had.
Now I like myself better since I started to see
That I was lousy being great – I'm much better being me.

What is your takeaway from this poem?

Self-Discovery Reflections

"How do you respond when people throw figurative darts at you in life? Here are a few suggestions: (1) Evaluate the situation objectively; (2) Stick to your principles and values; and (3) Double-down in your self-belief."

Ben Loeb

"Success is not final; Failure is not fatal: It is the courage to continue that counts."

Winston S. Churchill

"The purpose of life is to live it, to taste experience to the utmost, to reach out eagerly and without fear for newer and richer experience."

Eleanor Roosevelt

CHAPTER 10

INVENTORIES

Introduction to Inventories

The "*What*":

A series of questionnaires that will give you more self-awareness in how to improve your mental performance skills.

The "*Why*":

To give the athlete the opportunity for self-evaluation which creates an opportunity for goal setting leading to self-improvement.

The "*How*":

Take each of the inventories in this chapter on different days. You could choose to do one a day, two a week, or one a week. You may decide to do them in the pre-competitive season, during the season, in the off-season, or a combination of those time periods.

The following exercises will only be beneficial of you reflect on them and then act. These exercises create the opportunity for self-discovery.

It's up to you to implement what you discover about yourself from the exercises to improve your mental performance skills.

Three Questions for Mental Performance

Score each question below (scale of 1 low- 10 high).
Circle your number and fill in the blank.

To what degree:

1. Do you look for solutions or do you become mentally absorbed in the problems?

1   **2**   **3**   **4**   **5**   **6**   **7**   **8**   **9**   **10**

Absorbed   **Look for**
by the problem   **a solution**

Resilience Score _____

2. Do you utilize on-court/field visualization and positive self-talk to focus on what you want to happen (capable of happening) vs what you are concerned might happen (negative occurrence)?

1   **2**   **3**   **4**   **5**   **6**   **7**   **8**   **9**   **10**

Negative   **Positive**
Visualization   **Visualization**
and Self-talk   **and Self-talk**

Confidence Score _____

3. Do you use breath control to positively influence your emotional state (i.e., stress, nervousness, relaxation)?

1   **2**   **3**   **4**   **5**   **6**   **7**   **8**   **9**   **10**

Low Emotional   **High Emotional**
Management State   **Management State**

Emotional Management Score _____

Total Score _______

**Discuss with a teammate or coach ways to improve
a particular score.**

Competitive Adjective Profile[25]

Fill in each blank below with a score for comparing the two adjectives on a 10-point scale.

1	2	3	4	5	6	7	8	9	10	Score
Fearful									Bold	____
Moody									Even Tempered	____
Non-Competitive									Competitive	____
Dependent									Self-Reliant	____
Uncommitted									Committed	____
Passive									Aggressive	____
Insecure									Confident	____
Undisciplined									Disciplined	____
Pessimistic									Optimistic	____
Unrealistic									Realistic	____
Uncoachable									Coachable	____
Immature									Mature	____
Porr Problem-Solver									Problem-Solver	____
Poor Team Player									Team Player	____
Unwilling to Take Risks									Take Risks	____
									Total Score	____
									Percentile Score	____

25 The 15 categories come from the Competitive Adjective Profile created by Jim Loehr, 1987.

Calculate the percentile score by taking your total score divided by 150 (max points).

For instance, if your score is 117 then 117/150 = 78% is your percentile score.

Compare your percentile score with that of a teammate.

Discuss your general observations and any specific adjectives that you see as a strength and an area that needs improvement.

What action can you take to improve in one or two categories?

Philosophical Beliefs for the Competitive Athlete[26]

What's the greatest feeling in competitive sports? (rank order)
1. To play (enjoy the feeling of playing the game)
2. To play for others (team)
3. Do it well
4. Winning

What is your rank order?

How can factors #1-3 affect winning?

Coach Patton's Six Principles to Instill in Players:

Score yourself 1 (low) to 10 (high) on each principle on how it relates to you with your competitive pursuits:
1. Joy (happiness; self-worth; value)   ______
2. Compassion for others (teammates)   ______
3. Passion (enthusiasm)   ______
4. Mindfulness (be fully present; emotionally non-judgmental)   ______
5. Gratitude (thankful for the opportunities in athletics and life)   ______
6. Competition (embrace it)   ______

Total Score ______

26 Greg Patton, Boise State University Men's Tennis Coach, Illinois Tennis Coaches Workshop; January 2017

Compare your total score with others on your team. Discuss with your teammate or coach.

Identify a principle you want to focus on in the coming weeks to improve upon or monitor. Be intentional in your effort to do so each day.

Why Do You Play Competitive Sports?

Place in rank order your first three choices among the 10 choices given for why you play competitive sports. Place a '1", "2", and a '3' in the blanks provided. **Read all choices before you decide on your responses**.

_____ Fitness

_____ Sport-specific skill development

_____ Develop self-discipline

_____ Improve self-esteem

_____ Accept responsibility

_____ Manage adversity/learn to solve problems

_____ Learn to win graciously and lose with honor

_____ To win

_____ The challenge of competing

_____ Have fun

Personal Mission Statement: this is a "life statement" that explains what you are about as you perform in this sport; it reflects how you want other people to see you. How do you want to be remembered? You may think of it as your primary reason for competing that goes deeper than your desire to win.

Personal Mission Statement:

Share your top 3 choices and your personal mission statement with a coach, teammate, or friend.

Why Do You Compete?[27]

Step 1

Circle the descriptor that more applies to you for each line below because of exposure to your sport:

Like yourself more	Like yourself less
More positive as a person	More negative as a person
More constructive inner voice	Less constructive inner voice
Greater self-confidence	Less self-confidence
Happier	Less happy
More focused	Less focused
More stable	More fragile
Less fearful	More fearful
Stronger character	Weaker character
More self-directed	Less self-directed
More humble	Bigger ego
More open to criticism	More defensive
More respectful of others	Less respectful of others
More disciplined	Less disciplined
More emotionally resilient	Less emotionally resilient
Love life more	Love life less
More grateful	Less grateful
Physically healthier	Phyiscally less healthy (i.e. injured)
More ethical	Less ethical
More energetic	Less energetic
More excited about life	Less ecited about life

27 Adapted from the Human Performance Institute, a division of Johnson &Johnson Health and Wellness Solutions, Inc. *(from their Mental Toughness Training Program)*

Step 2

Write your answers to the questions below and then discuss with a coach or teammate.

1. How can competition help you in your journey towards being the person you want to become?
2. What is the potential negative consequence of using sport performance to build your self-esteem and self-value?
3. How would you define personal success as an athlete?

Self-Evaluation & Goal Setting for Sport Achievement

Player/Athlete Strengths:

Physical -

Mental/Emotional -

Areas for Improvement:

Physical -

Mental/Emotional -

Fears:

Aspirations (aspire to achieve):

Practice or Performance Goals for Personal Improvement:

Outcome Goals (optional):

Grit Inventory

How "gritty" are you as an athlete? Think of grit as your level of passion and your ability to persevere when the going gets tough. Do you exhibit the skills to stay with it for the long-term to overcome the obstacles and meet your goal?

Directions for taking the *Grit Inventory Questionnaire*:
Respond to the following ten items. Respond as it applies to your competitive arena. Be honest there are no right or wrong answers! Use the following choices to choose your response. Put your answer in the blank after each question.

Scoring Scale:
**5: Very much like me 4: Mostly like me 3: Somewhat like me
2: Not much like me 1: Not at all like me**

1. Setbacks during the competition don't discourage me. ____
2. I am resilient in my ability to overcome losses and remain determined moving forward. ____
3. Success during the competition does not lower my intensity level. ____
4. I am comfortable with new coaching ideas and trying something different. ____
5. My interest in my sport stays steady and does not fluctuate during the season. ____
6. My commitment level stays steady and does not diminish during the season. ____
7. I set goals before the season, monitor my progress, and stick to them. ____

8. I am able to maintain my focus and a desire to compete over the entire season. ____

9. I am the type of person who will always finish the season once it's started, no matter where I fit in on the team. ____

10. I am passionate about my involvement in my competitive arena (sport). ____

Total Score for Questions #1-10: ____

Average Score= Total Score/10 (round to nearest tenth): ____

Average Score Range:
4.5-5.0 Extremely Gritty; 3.5-4.5 Mostly Gritty
2.5-3.5 Somewhat Gritty; 1.5-2.5 Not Very Gritty;
1.0-1.5 Not At All Gritty

Discuss your responses to the following questions with a teammate or your coach:

1. Would you consider your score a fair assessment of your "grit" in competitive athletics?

2. **ACTION PLAN:** What should you do if there is a *"grit" deficiency* in your performance arena?

3. What are some key factors if *grit* is a *personal strength*?

Core Values of a Successful Athlete

The United States Tennis Association has a high-performance division led by Dr. Larry Lauer. He and national coaches of the USTA Player Development developed seven core values of successful players. The seven core values can be applied to any athlete.

Listed below are the 7 core values:

Rate yourself on a scale of 1 to 5 (1 = Low, 3 = Average, 5 = High) on each core value in the blank that follows each core value.

1. **Confidence** - players must have an unshakable self-belief in their abilities and skills. _____
2. **Determined** - players push through hardship and struggle while continuing to strive for success in a positive way. _____
3. **Engaged** - players should have their full focus directed on what matters in that particular moment. _____
4. **Professional** - players should demonstrate good character and exhibit the behavior and attitude of an athlete who is consistently prepared to practice and compete with full engagement. _____
5. **Resilient** - players should show they can bounce back and refocus after failures, letdowns, etc., and bring their best effort to the next point (or play in some sports). _____
6. **Respectful** - players should act in a way that demonstrates appreciation for the game, respect to opponents and teammates, while demonstrat-

ing sportsmanship and honoring the rules of
the game. _____

7. **Tough** - players must be able to endure periods of difficulty and adversity in training and in competition, both mentally and physically. _____

Exercise:

1. Discuss your scores for each core value with a teammate or with your coach.

2. Which one or two core values do you see as a real **strength**?

3. Which one or two core values do you see as an area you want to **improve upon**?

4. What **plan of action** will you take to improve upon those core values in # 3?

5. **Discuss your plan of action** with a teammate or a coach.

Winning Strategies for Personal Performance[28]

Four Questions to ask yourself after each performance (i.e., match or game)

Grade Yourself on a scale of 1 (low) to 10 (high)

1. Did you give your absolute best effort? ____
2. Did you embrace problems and look for a way to solve them? ____
3. Did you create "play frames" (visualize the ebbs & flows) in a way to promote constructive focus and confidence? ____
4. Did you sustain a predominately positive attitude with yourself no matter what happened? ____

Total Score ____

Share your scores with a teammate or a coach and then discuss ways you can improve your mental skill for a given question.

28 Dr. James Loehr

Identify Your Mental Weapons

The following self-evaluation inventory comes courtesy of Larry Lauer, director of mental skills with the USTA.[29]

Scoring guide: 1 = poor/low at the skill; 2 = below average; 3 = average at the skill; 4 = above average/good; 5= very good/great at the skill. Rate yourself on a scale of 1 to 5.

	Mental Skill/Characteristic	Score
1.	Confidence in abilities	______
2.	Motivation to practice/train	______
3.	Desire; give full effort in competition	______
4.	Focus during competition	______
s.	Ability to refocus after mistakes	______
6.	Set goals that drive training and performances	______
7.	Positive during competition	______
8.	Manage stress well during competition	______
9.	Control emotions during competition	______
10.	Ability to relax when nervous	______
11.	Exhibit positive body language/posture during competition	______
12.	Use mental imagery effectively	______
1 3.	Use routines effectively during competition	______
14.	Prepared for competition	______
15.	Practice with intensity	______
	Mental Composite Index (MCI) Total Score	______

---

29 From the article "Learn Your Strengths and ID Your Mental Weapons."

Now that you have taken stock of your mental game, it is important to do the following:

1. Compare your Mental Composite Index (Total Score) to the following scale to get an overall mental score.

   Total MCI Score =15-21 Poor; 22-36 Below average; 37-50 Average; 51-60 Above average; 61-68 Very good; 69-75 Outstanding. Circle the descriptor that is associated with your score.

2. List two of your mental weapons you can rely on when you compete. For instance, if your mental weapon is being positive, use your positive thinking during games to overcome mistakes and to stay focused on the task at hand.

3. Assess two of your lower scores and write a statement on how you will improve these mental skills.

The Second, Un-demanded Mile

Reflect on your preparation and training in your performance arena.

On a scale of 1-10 (1 low; 5 average, 10 high), **rate yourself** on the following for each category (circle the appropriate number):

Low				Average					High
1	2	3	4	5	6	7	8	9	10

The overall **intensity** of your training

Low				Average					High
1	2	3	4	5	6	7	8	9	10

The degree to which you **take the initiative** without a coach directive.

Low				Average					High
1	2	3	4	5	6	7	8	9	10

The willingness to **persevere** during demanding phases of your training.

Low				Average					High
1	2	3	4	5	6	7	8	9	10

The willingness to be **resilient** when things are not going your way in your training.

Low				Average					High
1	2	3	4	5	6	7	8	9	10

The level of **confidence** your training will pay off in noticeable improvement.

Calculate your **Second, Un-demanded Mile Total Score** = ______

Compare your individual scores and total score with a teammate or coach by discussing **ways to attain a high score in each category**. An alternative is to write down a response or type your response onto a word document.

The Iceberg Illusion

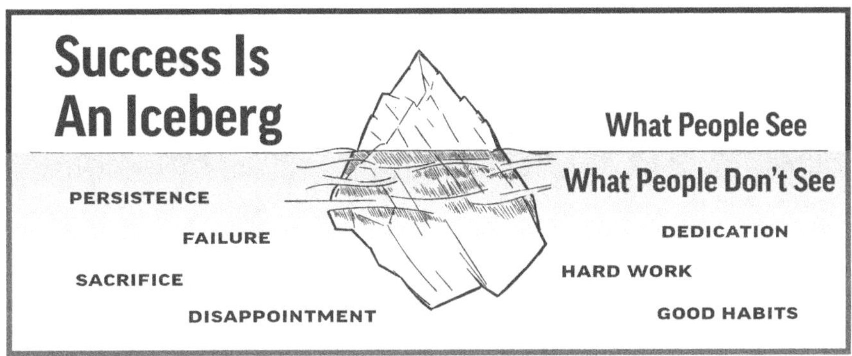

Each athlete should rank themselves on a scale of 1 (low/ not good) - 5 (high/good) on each of the following criteria that is "below the surface"? Rate yourself on the factors that create success.

Persistence	1	2	3	4	5
Dealing with Disappointment during the event	1	2	3	4	5
Dealing with Failure	1	2	3	4	5
Sacrifice - What are you willing to give up?	1	2	3	4	5
Dedication to meeting a goal	1	2	3	4	5
Hard Work	1	2	3	4	5
Good Habits/Responsible	1	2	3	4	5

List one thing you are willing to do, or do better, to strive to achieve a higher level of success. Then share with a coach or a teammate.

MORE FROM AUTHOR BEN LOEB, Ed. S.

Books

ACE Your Way: *100 Acronyms, Cue Statements, & Equations To Better Serve Your Life* (B. Loeb)

The Athlete's Playbook: *Building a Culture of Mental Toughness: The Pyramid Model* (R. McGuire, B. Loeb, A. Selking, P. Ivy)

Next Level Coaching: *How to Use Sport Psychology To Educate, Motivate, and Improve Student-Athlete Performance* (B. Loeb)

Videos

Tennis Instructional 3-Pack Video Series: *Best Team Tennis Practices* *(singles, doubles,* ***mental performance****); Championship Productions*

Major Publication Articles

Self-Awareness: An Internal Audit. Association for Applied Sport Psychology Blog, April 2024. https://appliedsportpsych.org/blog/2024/03/self-awareness-an-internal-audit/

Coaching Philosophy 101: *What Experience Can Teach You; International Journal of Coaching Science; July 2022*

ABOUT THE AUTHOR

Ben Loeb, Ed. S. (University of Missouri-Columbia) has been coaching tennis teams since 1986. He coached the women's tennis team at the University of Missouri from 1986-1988 while working on his graduate degree. In 1989 he started his high school coaching career at Hickman H. S. (Columbia, MO), where he coached the boys' and girls' teams. In the spring of 1994, the boys' team won the school's first and only tennis state championship. Coach Loeb started coaching the girls' team (fall 1994) and the boys' team (spring 1995) at Rock Bridge H S (Columbia, MO). The Rock Bridge teams have won 18 team state championships during his tenure. Coach Loeb has directed the high school teams he has coached to 43 Final Four appearances and more than 1,225 dual meet victories, which is a state record.

Ben also developed a sport psychology course for the high school level, one he taught from 2011 thru 2019. The course is still taught today at the high schools in the Columbia Public Schools district. Ben retired from teaching the course to focus on writing books that emphasized exercises and reflective thoughts to improve mental performance in athletics and in life. He has written four books including this one. In addition, Ben has directed and created the content for three tennis instructional videos (Championship Productions). One of the videos is on applying mental performance skills for the competitive tennis player.

Ben has presented at many different tennis coaching clinics, with the mental side of the game an area of emphasis. He has received many awards to honor his career. Some of them include: The St. Louis Tennis Hall of Fame (2024); The Missouri State H S Activities Association Distinguished Service Award (2022); National H S Tennis Coaches Assoc. Hall of Fame (2021); Don Faurot Sportsperson of the Year — Columbia, MO (2017); Missouri Sports Hall of Fame (2015). He lives in Columbia, Missouri, with his wife, Sarah, his son, Ben, and their beloved dog, Buddy.